Manufactured in United States of America
Library of Congress Cataloging-Publication Data
Mohberg, Noel
Management of Mousetrap R&D, by Noel Mohberg
284 p.
ISBN 978-0-9853308-1-1

Acknowledgements

This book has been a labor. It might never have been finished without the support and encouragement of the Richland Area Writer's Circle.

Special thanks to my three mentors are due: James Grizzle, PhD, the best professor ever, Richard Prairie, PhD, the best boss ever, and Merril Hume, PhD, the best friend ever. All three have been invaluable as mentors and as friends in my career.

MANAGEMENT

OF

MOUSETRAP R&D

Noel Mohberg

Management of Mousetrap R&D

Abbreviations and Acronyms

admin	Administrative assistant
BS&P	Business Systems & Procedures
BM	Beginning Management
CHWDRHD	Corporate Head, Worldwide Department of Resources and Human Development
CV	Curriculum Vitae
CTA	Cover Thine Ass
DA	Desert Aromatics (Inc)
DAPAC	Desert Aromatics Political Action Committee
DMWT	Deputy Management Workshop Trainer
DP	Dilbert Principle
DoD	Department of Defense
GAO	General Accounting Office
GRPAC	Grass Roots Political Action Committee
HR	Human Resources
KNAFE	Knows Not Ass from Elbow
OA	Over Achiever
org	Organization
PP	Peter Principle
R&D	Research and Development
SAASS	Senior Aine-Allee Systems Specialist
SOP	Standard Operating Procedure
VVA	Vestal Virgins of America
USAF	United States Air Force
WNKR	Workshop Note Keeper-Recorder

Introduction

What's this with "Mousetrap R&D"?

According to the sage of ages Ralph Waldo Emerson, if you build a better mouse trap, the world will beat a path to your door. This slogan has been used thousands of times to justify creation of new products. It's the ultimate testimonial. But is it true? Actually, no. Emerson didn't write word one about mousetraps. Further:

a) Mousetraps are cheap, low profit, commodity items.

b) The mouse control industry is rife with competition from poisons and exterminators.

c) There are a zillion kinds of mousetraps on the market.

d) Inventing mousetraps is among the least likely of all endeavors to be profitable.

According to Ballis[1], The Little Nipper, patented in 1898, dominates (like 60%) the world market. In the history of the US Patent Office, approximately 4,400 mousetrap patents have been granted. Of these, about 20 (0.45%) were profitable.

These are way worse odds than playing the ponies or casino gambling, and in casinos, we losers get free drinks. Plus, we take no flak from the mousey huggers and we can deduct gambling loses from winnings if we ever hit a jackpot.

---

[1] Ballis, Mary. "History of the Mousetrap." ThoughtCo, June 20, 2017, Thoughtco.com

So, yes, indeed, you got it right. Mousetrap R&D is a dorky title. But mousetrap research and development is a dorky caricature of R&D, and it follows that this is a dorky caricature of management books.

What's so special about this book?

There is an epidemic of management advice in the media. Online schools offer innumerable options for executive training and honing management skills. We are besieged from all eighths[2] by talking heads who claim to know far better than we how to manage our work, our play, and even our most intimate relationships.

Business management curricula flourish on our college campuses, employing untold numbers of professors. Although few of these professors ever actually manage anything, it's possible that some are actually competent to instruct others in management. Surely many curricula provide useful training in specific business skills, such as accounting and tax law. No doubt, too, the lion's share of management training programs are useful, but not all programs are chock-full of help for the aspiring real-world manager.

---

[2] Besieged from all eighths—situations twice as dire as besieged from all quarters.

For example, in 1998, my company sent me to a one-week advanced (i.e., non-remedial) management course at a prestigious university[3]. This blue-ribbon course was taught by a full professor, cost my company a bundle, and the only useful thing I learned was that if I started at the blossom end of the banana, it would peel easier than if I started at the stem end. The drawback with the blossom end tactic is that the sniglets[4] don't come off as neatly. I had to learn that on my own, though.

Competency aside, it seems that half of all business school professors have written a sanctimonious tome on management. Almost every bookstore in our beloved land has scores of volumes on management. So, this book is just an **Oh-Crap-Not-Another!** management book. It's even less likely to enhance your management skill set than my banana-peeling professor, or for that matter, just about any other book.

Why is this book needed?

So why is this book needed? The short answer is, "It isn't." The long answer is, "Of course, it isn't. Any fool can see that." The really long answer is that if this book is needed at all, it's because it covers topics not to be found in other management books.

---

[3] Hint: In Ann Arbor, the school is called "The Harvard of the Midwest". In East Lansing, it's called "The Harvard of Washtenaw County".
[4] Sniglets are the little stringy boppers that cling to the banana flesh while you are peeling it. They taste like the peeling, only not as good.

This book provides guidance on hardcore issues, such as rumor management, what to do if your boss does performance reviews at a topless bar, words for writing a performance review that sounds great but means nothing, and how to manage your manager.

But what is "Management"?

Good grief! It's only page twelve and I'm already ahead of myself. Implicit in the text above is the assumption that everybody knows what management is. You ask a dozen people to define management, though, and you get a dozen different answers. So, before I get any further, I'd best clarify my terms. For a broad definition, I appeal to Wikipedia, the universal gold standard for terminology and just about everything else.

> *"**Management in businesses and organizations** is the function that coordinates the efforts of people to accomplish goals and objectives by using available resources efficiently and effectively. Management includes planning, organizing, staffing, leading or directing, and controlling an organization to accomplish the goal or target."*

As broad definitions go, this is fine, but this book isn't about broads at all. It's about what you do to induce a dude to do a task not of his choosing while being allowed to use less than optimal resources and conforming to arbitrary rules of engagement. Further, if the dude fails at the task, management covers your options for fixing things as well as choices if the dude needs fixing, too.

Format, language and such

This book is organized by Chapters. Within Chapters there is a single topic. There is an expository section heading each topic, followed by an allegedly relevant case study. Almost as if this was a real management book, teaching moment lessons are noted in the case studies. Remarks intended to clarify or amplify the lessons are scattered about.

Well, yes, some of the remarks are intended to mislead you as well. You'll know them when you see them, though. In fact, most of this book is satiric nonsense, but here and there passages of management dogma are regurgitated. To spare the astute who doubt that there are differences between dogma and nonsense, the dogma is shown with a shaded background.

The other thing is footnotes. You may ignore them, but don't. I like footnotes because they make the book appear to be authoritative when it isn't and allow me to work in a gag without disrupting the text flow.

I have chosen to write this in barnyard vernacular to remind the reader now and again that this is not a mainstream management book.

I'm reluctant to accept all the blame for this book, so from this point forward, "we" employ the royal we. And, since "you" has three letters while "dear esteemed reader" takes twenty spaces and "friends and collegial kinfolk" has a marginally unacceptable acronym, the text is addressed to "you".

Sources

We served twenty-odd years in entry-level-go-directly-to-terminal R&D management, making more than our fair share of errors. However, when we exchanged anecdotes with other managers, we found they often had stunningly similar tribulations and comparably dreadful success/failure ratios. Our late-night conversations were veritable cornucopias of mistakes and missteps. Our counterparts had such a wealth of woes that we have been able to draw nearly all our case studies from their and not our banks of memorably regretful experiences.

The setting

Drawing on others' experiences as case studies presents a problem. How can we span the wide spectrum of the contexts of their experiences in beaucoup situations at dozens of companies?

Since it's way harder to move mountains than Moses, we've transported all their quandaries into the context of a single fictitious company.

Real management books feature case studies of generic people performing generic tasks at hypothetical operations that make widgets. Common, ordinary widgets. Well, okay, maybe some of them now make the advanced Mark VII model, but it's still just nothing but a damn widget.

But simply building widgets is too confining for us, so we've created a whole company named Desert Aromatics (DA). The hypothetical mission of DA is not merely manufacturing widgets; its mission is hypobolically hyperthetical because DA does only super-secret classified military work.

The characters

Populating these case studies is a fixed troupe of characters who are like escapees from a comic strip—that is, they never age, never learn, and always stay in character until the author writes them out. It's incredulous but cut us a little slack here. Your upside is that there's no need to get acquainted with a new set of jerks for each new topic. Once you learn about John and Bernie in Chapter 1, you don't have to suffer through their descriptions again. Saves us ink and you, aggravation.

The primary protagonist is John Smith, an exceptionally unexceptional type such as is commonly found in the lower management strata in techie fields. He doesn't look, act, or sound like an alpha guy and is known to vanish into the crowd when there are but three people in the room. John lacks the social graces and personal charisma requisite for a career in either accounting or engineering, and although he tested out in the 95th percentile on the Mortician Aptitude Exam, he chose a college major in computerese.

A star at data collection and data management but neither trained nor inclined to manage people, John was the only available computer science geek so he began as the pup snatched from the litter and anointed as the leader of a staff of on-the-job-trained, self-accredited computer nerds. From the moment of taking his seat behind the desk in that private but windowless, entry-level manager's confines until late in the afternoon of his retirement day, John is doomed to quietly toil, ever appearing to be overmatched by the duties of his office.

John's boss is Bernie. Rejoice if you've never had to work for Bernie. Lawrence, Cyrus, and Maurice are John's fellow minor managers. Lawrence smiles constantly, Cy is bald and cunning, and Maurice is, um—Maurice. Della is Bernie's administrative assistant (admin), gofer, snitch, and enabler.

Why are all the managers men?

Proper management books feature managers of neutral gender named Chris and Fran and Kelly. This is not a proper management book.

When we started working for a living in the unenlightened '60s, 90% of our colleagues were males and this was in the women-had-to-be-twice-as-good-to-get-promoted-half-as-quickly era. As a result, the few women in management were exceptionally strong and made few errors. Since dumb-ass mistakes make the best stories, we got almost no material about female managers. Hence, we have written this as if all the managers were males. Besides:

a) This book makes no claim to being politically correct.
b) We have data. Of the 318 Darwin Award[5] nominees from '95 to '14, 282 (88.7%) were males.
c) Bernie was a male chauvinist pig who would not consider a female manager.
d) Using "they" as a gender neutral singular personal pronoun pains our prehistoric English grammar trained souls. He/she/it is error-prone[6].
e) Replacing male terms by their female equivalents in this book will make a bunch of women sound like dolts, too. Do you really want that?

Outside the box versus beneath the box

Management literature calls for thinking of outside-the-box problem solutions. This book carries that concept further; it calls for thinking of beneath-the-box problem solutions. Some of these solutions are cunning, some crass, others are evil, and one or two are diabolically charming.

How to read this book

This book is best read as you'd sip a fine liqueur. Friend Jim said it best: "Love your writing. I keep your book on the night stand and read one chapter every night. Puts me right to sleep."

---

[5] Darwin Awards are given annually for individuals who serve society by removing themselves from the human gene pool through acts of exceptional stupidity. See Wikipedia.
[6] The term "he/she/it" is clumsy and too easily written "he/sheit".

Summary

This book is a poor man's situation comedy, lacking only the ads, the laugh track, and the video. Wisdom is trumped by expediency, futility is the order of the day, and inanity is everywhere.

The case studies are inspired by real life conflicts, but when groups of managers lament, a good story takes on a life of its own. So, instead of sacrosanct, it's an adventure at and around Dilbert's Point of Parody Inversion[7].

A warning

Should you attempt to utilize an idea from this book, you must realize that this will be done at your own risk and in peril of culpability of high crime. This book's mission is to entertain you. It won't enlighten you. It might endarken you, though.

---

[7] Dilbert's Parody Inversion Point is the moment when parody becomes reality and reality becomes parody. See Dilbert, 10/02/2019.

Have you read the Introduction? If yes, proceed. If you have not, either read it or put this book back on the shelf. This book will annoy you if you don't read the Intro.

Chapter 1

Company Goals

From lofty corporate suites to the dustiest broom closets in shabby outbuildings, company goals drive management's every voice and choice. "Hit these objectives and we'll succeed!" they avow. At least that is what's written in the annual report to stockholders.

Since these goals must be ultra-critical to success, we'll start this book here. Neil Armstrong's journey to the moon began by getting out of bed and taking his first step toward the toilet. Commensurate with his small first step, this chapter considers the impact of entry-level management on company decisions.

Case Study

Fresh out of the US Air Force (USAF) and holding a Master's in Business Systems and Procedures[8] (BS&P) from a third-rate college, John hired into a black box job at Taytes Navigation Instruments in Albuquerque.

---

[8] These days, a Master's in Business Systems and Procedures might be called an MBA with emphasis in Information Science, but then it was just BS with P.

Taytes, a shadowy operation with a history of contracting Department of Defense (DoD) work, had just spun out from a larger and even murkier aircraft, Wisconsin cheese, off-shore oil, medical device, and unisex hygiene products conglomerate. Flexing their newly semi-independent muscles, Taytes was in the hunt for new projects and new staff.

Before he stepped in the Taytes door, John knew only the salary he'd accepted and that Taytes worked on classified military applications. His lack of understanding could have been attributed to Taytes' overreaching cloak of need-to-know secrecy. Or maybe John was a little oblivious and a slow learner. His failure to ask the key questions at the employment interview didn't help, either.

On his first day at work, John learned that he would not be just *in* BS&P at Taytes. He—sock, jock, and underarmor—would *be* BS&P at Taytes. Although he had no support staff, he was promised access to an IBM 1620 computer in the Taytes salvage and refit warehouse. He alone was to be accountable for all data systems and analysis support for whatever projects were under contract.

For John, this was a dream job. He was going from gofer to guy in charge. Instead of running for a coffee with no sugar and two creams, he'd be running the show.

John's first on-the-job orientation meeting was with his boss Jim, the manager of Engineering Support Systems. Jim's pleasant, easy-going manner lasted until John asked about Bernie, whose name appeared above Jim's on the organization (org) chart.

Jim's eyes narrowed. "Oh my God! Didn't anybody warn you about **Bernie**?" —pause— "Nooo. I suppose they didn't. Bernie has everybody scared shitless, and HR[9] is convinced we'd never fill another opening in his department if anybody said…"

Jim's voice fell to a whisper as beads of sweat broke out on his forehead. "You gotta stay on his good side. Annoy him and he'll crush you like a mosquito. Get off on the wrong foot with him and he might amputate it. He seldom forgives and never forgets. If you cross him, he'll pull strings and ruin your career. I've seen it happen. He's got half the R&D shop managers in Albuquerque by the short hairs and even some Pentagon brass owe him favors."

John's orientation meeting that afternoon was with Mathew. He was the Manager of Redevelopment[10] Engineering. His take on Bernie was, in its way, even more frightening. "Sure, Bernie is scary, but you have to understand these things. He's like the Dean of Men in a college who meets only two kinds of students; the suck-ups and the—um—mess-ups. Bernie is told exactly what he wants to hear except when he hears exactly what he doesn't want to hear. And Bernie knows how handle the mess-ups."

A day or two later, John viewed the maze of Taytes Instrument Company contracts in need of BS&P support. Surprisingly, there were zero navigational instrument projects.

---

[9] HR is Human Resources, not Humane Resources or Help Resources
[10] Cynics might allege that Redevelopment Engineering is Patent Piracy Engineering (PPE). Not so; the PPE guys are into reverse engineering while the Redevelopment engineers evade patent law by artfully tweaking parallel processes.

"There's been a reliability problem," Jim said, "the company trashed their last gyro horizon a year ago. Word got onto the street that 'he who has a Taytes is lost'."

At the general staff meeting on Friday, Bernie showed off his artistic skill with a euphemism whitewash brush. Although every one of Taytes' twenty-odd contracts involved components that were destined to end up in weapons, Bernie insisted that Taytes' corporate mission was "Building a Better Mousetrap".

John's first project was an altitude sensor. He supposed the sensor might end up in an air burst bomb like the one featured in a **Mechanics Illustrated** article. It speculated on the bomb's likely performance in Viet Nam; enemy, water buffalos, chickens, and fish, beware! John figured it would be hell on mosquitoes, too, but the DoD funded no research in insect control.

Without the promised computer but being an able and loyal employee, John forged ahead with his tasks. Using only pen and paper, he somehow completed his assignments ahead of schedule. And, of course, with this success things got far worse. He was promptly assigned to a larger and far uglier task.

Lesson 1.1: This a widely utilized and very successful management tactic. If a guy stars at an ugly task, promptly reward him with a small bonus[11] and assignment to several even uglier tasks.

---

[11] Bonuses carry higher esteem than raises. However, bonuses cost way less than raises over the long haul because bonuses don't increase the base salary.

John's second "mousetrap" was a detonator such as used in a land mine. This device was designed to lie inertly for variable times of up to a month before the electronic trigger self-activated. After the activation, any vibration[12] would fire the detonator.

But a wee problem arose. Static electricity activated the triggers, too. The Taytes mousetrap/DoD detonator project was canceled when no way was found to completely quell the static electricity.

Bernie was undeterred. Thinking there must be more mousetraps needing Taytes' R&D tweaking, he rode the staff ever harder as they scoured the DoD bid opportunities.

John responded to Bernie's new contract demands by stepping back to look at the broader perspective.

While Bernie harangued, John reflected. Wars were mostly fought, he thought, by burgeoning populations competing for scarce resources. All wars were terribly expensive, but wars on terrorism were the costliest because they go on for years and years — the anti-terrorists need to kill the terrorists, then revenge-seeking spouses, and finally wipe out their offspring as they feather out as 12-year-old terrorists.

John reasoned that in Viet Nam instead of killing, stemming population growth should be the real goal. He was sure that biological mechanisms would be far more effective than wars for terrorist prevention.

---

[12] The weapons design guys bragged that a blue damselfly could safely perch on an activated detonator, but hummingbirds would get blown out of the air if they flew over and crapped at the wrong time.

With his concept translated into Bernie's vernacular, "With a better cat, just imagine the savings on Mousetrap R&D!" and without checking with Jim, John went to Bernie's office. Della was in the ladies' room, so John just appeared in Bernie's doorway.

Bernie looked up, studied John for a moment, and then politely asked, "What in hell do you want?"

John blurted out, "I'm John Smith from BS&P and I've come to present a revolutionary idea for Mousetrap R&D." Without waiting for Bernie's approval to go ahead, John raced through his alternative approach to dealing with terrorists.

John's idea went like this: Wherever the enemy controls the territory, the US forces offer contraception with intrauterine devices in exchange for furloughs from napalm attacks, spraying Agent Orange on their rice paddies, and carpet-bombing their homes and fields. The medical device arm of the parent company then ups their game by bidding on the DoD contract for contraceptive devices.

John's talk took less than a minute.

Bernie sat in silence. His body language suggested a certain hesitancy regarding John's proposal, though. The smile that flitted across Bernie's face turned into a glow.

Ah, good, John thought, Bernie understood.

"So. You claim to be **Mister Smith** from BS&P. Well, I don't know any Smiths and I'm not sure what BS&P is," Bernie explained, his voice and tone as mellifluous as Senator Everett Dirksen's, "but you are **despicable!** Your idea is savage, immoral, loathsome, and hate-filled. Birth control is fiendish and utterly unchristian. It promotes **fornication. You are fired.**"

John fled to Jim's office. That didn't go well, either. "He thought Smith was a phony name. How can he fire me if he doesn't even know my name?" John lamented.

"Bernie's the company rainmaker," Jim said. "If he didn't know your name, you caught a huge break. If you were a good-looking woman, he'd know your name, marital status, and cup size, but for him, guys are just faces in the crowd." Jim paused. "Now, before he and Della figure out that you are actually John Smith and Della calls Security on you, I'll walk you the guard gate."

Thus ended John's brief Taytes Instruments career.

Lesson 1.2: What we've got here is a failure to communicate.

Remark: John's vision of success was winning the war, but Bernie's concept of success was Taytes turning a large profit. It's different in context but similar in effect to The Captain leaving Cool Hand Luke a beaten, smashed pulp in the ditch and telling the rest of the prisoners, "What we've got here is a failure to communicate."

Lesson 1.3: In the for-profit world, most business decisions are driven by profit potential, a few by potentially enhanced prestige, and a very few by potential benefit to the consumers.

Remark: It's not so different in the non-profit/public sector. Most public service decisions are driven by the availability of funding, a few are driven by needs for show, and almost none by a potential benefit to consumers who have no lobbyists.

Lesson 1.4: Since senior managers believe they get paid to think of Good Big Ideas, they tend to think that everybody else thinks of Mediocre Little Ideas or Bad Big Ideas.

Remark: Senior managers welcome junior managers' alternative ideas regarding corporate goals in the same way that we in the peasant class welcome hornets and fire ants at picnics.

In the absence of a truly startling realignment of heavenly bodies, a minor manager doesn't stand one chance in hell of redirecting corporate goals toward his special concern. If you have a Big Idea and want to work on that idea, go find a company that is already pursuing the idea. If you want to be sure to work on your cherished idea, you'll have to start your own company.

But. Should you decide to take a stand and go toe-to-toe to advocate your cause within your company, there are two issues to consider:

- Your courage will get you a batch of likes on your Facebook page. However, should your demands rock the company canoe, your demands will cost you more friends than your grit will gain you.
- If you're sure that your higher calling in life is serving as shit on the company shoelace[13], you will need an independent source of income. Inheritances or sugar mommy allowances are good sources.

---

[13] Gotta be careful about shoe laces. Shit on a shoelace is a super stealth presentation. Brown on brown or black will be smelled before seen.

Where does John go from here?

So, what's to become of our unemployed John, you wonder.

John has no sugar mommy or trust fund. What he has is his ex-wife Blanche and her two kids, whom he has legally adopted. What Blanche has is a lawyer with hatred in his heart, greed in his soul, and a tame judge in his pocket. And the judge has an issued decree that John cannot move out of state until both kids no longer need child support.

The only employer in Albuquerque who will hire John is Desert Aromatics[14], Inc. (DA). For a time, this appears to be a big break for John because this job is a better fit than the Taytes job ever was. Within months he emerges as their best BS&P guy, so he is promoted to minimal management as the head of a fledgling four-man BS&P section.

But now lightning strikes. The DA Brass Balls hire Bernie away from Taytes to become DA's Big Kahuna in Contract Acquisitions and Operations. And John's new boss. John is right back in bed with Bernie. But for John, DA is the only game in town, so John is now shackled to the bedstead.

---

[14] Desert Aromatics originated as a company specializing in military gas dispersion technology. After just a few minor nerve gas mishaps, DA branched out into general military applications.

Chapter 2

The Performance Review

Almost any management book will provide appropriate guidance for doing performance reviews in non-contentious situations. Hence, although these routine cases are the great majority, we feel no need to consider this class of reviews because they are so well covered elsewhere. This chapter considers only the more challenging performance review situations.

First, a little homage to the system:

The annual performance review process is the pinnacle event in the manager/subordinate relationship. This review typically involves three phases; the preparation phase for both the manager and the subordinate, the face-to-face interview phase, and the manager's documentation phase to summarize accomplishments and plan future tasks.

Preparation phase

Caricatures of performance review preparations usually feature a boss weaponizing himself with probing questions aimed at each of the subordinate's shortcomings. The subordinate will be depicted as girding up his loins with excuses and alibis for every failing his boss might cite. Some will claim that this is not a caricature.

But what if this caricature is the best-case scenario? Subordinates sometimes argue that the Sixth Amendment[15] gives them the right to "no surprises" in performance reviews. But "no surprises" means "no unpleasant surprises" and the problem with no unpleasant surprises is that the guy in line for an Oh Crap! level surprise is typically non-self-critical and oblivious of his job's nuances.

Most managers think that learning the ins and outs of the job are integral parts of the subordinate's accountability and that the manager should not have to routinely tell the subordinate what to do. Further, the manager should almost never need to tell the subordinate how to do routine tasks. In general, unpleasant surprises will ensue when the subordinate's and manager's senses of tasks and priorities do not exist in the same universe.

Interview Phase

There is greater need for clear and concise manager/subordinate communications in the employee performance interview than in any other management function. The interview must focus on giving the subordinate an exact and clear evaluation of his status, his strengths, his weaknesses, and what is to be done about it all.

---

[15] Sixth Amendment—Speedy public trial, have a lawyer, confront witnesses, informed of charges, etc.

Most interviews go okay, but things tend to fall off if the subordinate is performing badly but thinks he's doing well. This leads to the manager assessing task performances as a series of monumental screw-ups, while the subordinate sees only rare shortfalls that are trivial issues of no greater consequence than losing a game of solitaire. The manager then concludes the subordinate is at best an incompetent clown, while the subordinate decides the manager is a hypercritical, prejudiced, and evil son of a bitch who makes snap judgments that are always incorrect and uniformly break against the subordinate.

All this makes things go badly at the interview. Even so, courtesy should prevail, as well as civility, tact, and reason. It doesn't always happen that way, though; communications have a way of breaking up like calls from a cheap cell phone on the far side of a tall mountain. Then, as the subordinate sees his career aspirations go down in flames, the manager may need to take steps to avoid physical confrontation. Should the interview further deteriorate into mortal conflict, the proactive manager will have resources in place to call 911.

Documentation Phase

The document summarizing the review process must be an accurate, precise, and balanced assessment of the subordinate's performance. The manager should come out of the review process with a better understanding of the subordinate's work and a finer grasp of what can be done to help the subordinate do a better job.

More commonly, it seems that the subordinate wants the review to be a flattering assessment of what he needs to do to get where he wants to go, while the manager writes the review as a series of steps designed to prevent any of the foregoing from happening.

Summary of phases

It's clear there may be bumps on the road to completed performance reviews. Communication might be less than ideal, the subordinate and manager may not be on the same page about the subordinate's tasks, or the subordinate's efforts may be tangential to management expectations. Lastly, the review document may have little to do with what the guy did or what the guy needs to do differently.

In the usual case, the interview is a one-on-one involving only the subordinate and manager, but witnesses may be present, and at times can be invaluable[16].

There is only one aspect of the performance review process that the manager can precisely control. It's the environment for conducting the interview. Performance interviews are as, or maybe even more, time and place dependent than any other managerial task. Hence, the setting should be chosen to be conducive to open and constructive communication. Distractions should be minimized and adequate time allowed to discuss all relevant issues.

---

[16] Invaluable as in the event of needing witness testimony, performing CPR, summoning an EMS/ELS Team, or ironing out any of a host of other wrinkles.

The case study below presents one example of an interesting choice of environment and circumstance for performance review interviews.

Case Study

Christmas time in Albuquerque is a festive time with the sunshine, the mountains all frosted with snow, and the blending of the Pueblo, Hispanic, and Anglo decoration traditions. Even John was in a festive mood until that fateful Monday afternoon in mid-December when he was summoned to Bernie's office.

A chill as cold as liquid nitrogen ran down John's spine. He feared the worst. It was performance review season, he was a green manager, and Bernie's big org chart still had a blank box above the BS&P Section where John's name belonged. Worse still, Bernie was Desert Aromatics' new broom who had, but a few months earlier, fired John from Taytes.

But, instead of a chewing out, it was an asking out. Bernie invited John to join him and the other managers at dinner on Friday. "I'm taking you guys out. It's a party, just for you managers. A purely social thing," Bernie promised. He stepped around the desk and raised his arm as if to put it around John's shoulders. But then he thought better of it and let the arm fall back down.

In his relief at hearing the invitation, John missed the retracted arm gesture. He left Bernie's office on top of the world. It would be John's first time as a managerial colleague in a social setting with Bernie. A managers' group dinner! It would be a fun time, but John cautioned himself about too much fun. He vowed to stay sober, and keep his mouth shut and eyes open.

The honeymoon effect was fleeting. Arriving five minutes early at the Monday afternoon managers' meeting, John took his usual seat just before the two senior managers Lawrence and Cyrus arrived. Lawrence's smile was thin and Cy's bald head glowed like a neon marquee. There were naught but dark and fearful words about the Christmas dinner, for Lawrence had a friend in management at Taytes. Bernie had a track record at Taytes' "purely social" managerial events. Lawrence asserted, and Cy agreed, that this Christmas dinner was the opening salvo for performance review season.

John was about to face a whole new set of hazards, for he knew from Taytes days that as tyrants go, Bernie starred. Being "reasonable" meant agreeing with him, "compromising" meant doing it his way, and "following orders" meant blindly doing it exactly his way. Bernie's staff meetings were tough, his managers' attaboy metings were punishment, and now John realized that performance review season was shaping up as exquisite torture.

On Tuesday morning John went to Bernie to say that he couldn't find a babysitter, so he'd have to pass on the invitation. But Bernie's invitation was a Godfather's offer; it couldn't be refused. "You are now part of **MY** leadership team," Bernie declared, "and I can't have a proper management team activity without you. If you want to continue working at DA, you **will** be there."

Frantic, John asked both Lawrence and Cy for guidance. Honorably enough, Lawrence and Cy sought to save their own asses, so they shared no specific fears. "Be careful about what you say," was the extent of their coaching.

John went to Maurice for advice. Maurice was a veteran who had bounced around the company and ended up as the CCTO[17]. Managers outranked CCs, so John outranked Mo—but this was only as a green second lieutenant outranks a grizzled top sergeant. Although Mo's management status was rumored to be shaky, John was unsure if he or Mo was the fourth leg of Bernie's three-legged stool. It mattered not; Mo gave no advice.

Other than to beware of bad things, John had no notion of what to expect from Bernie, the Jewish Mormon from Queens, New York. But being a little naïve, John resolved to invest in a babysitter and learn what could be learned. Since Bernie was picking up the check, Bernie got to call the shots. And all the whens, wheres, whats, whys, and hows.

All wearing suits and ties and Bernie in his wing-tip oxfords and resplendent in his polished-seat, navy blue, pin-stripe funeral and wedding suit, the group left work a half-hour early on Friday. Bernie drove, in his yellow Cadillac.

---

[17] Maurice was Crew Chief of Technical Operations—more or less techie-in-chief

Edie, the El Ranchito[18] hostess, must have known Bernie well because she greeted him by name and led the group to a booth in the darkest corner of the lounge. Bernie introduced the guys. "Edie, this is my management team — Larry, Curly, and Mo." — then a long pause — "And the new guy." So. It was true. Bernie had retained Maurice as a manager to fill a specific need.

Edie took orders for drinks. John ordered a gin and tonic with lots of tonic and lots of lime. He'd never been able to hold his booze so as Edie left the table, he excused himself and followed her, slipping her a couple bucks and asking that his drinks be very light on gin. She was happy enough to take the money, but the drink had teeth aplenty when it arrived.

Lesson 2.1: Although bribery can sometimes be surprisingly inexpensive and effective, it is not a completely reliable tool.

Remark: Even then, two bucks was not enough to make the bartender slack off on cheap booze — everybody knows that the drunker the guy, the bigger the tip.

Lesson 2.2: Trying to stay sober around the boss is always a good idea.

Remark: It's a really good idea if your boss is a Mormon.

---

[18] El Ranchito - a nearly topless bar and full Monty strip club. Locally pronounced "El Raunchito".

Bernie announced that since he was picking up the check, he had dibs on all the Old-Fashioned cherries, the martini olives, and the whisky sour orange slices. He didn't much care for limes, though, and advised John to change to a drink with better tasting fruit.

They all knew that because of osmotic pressure there was more alcohol in the fruit than in the rest of the drink, but only Mo felt the need to point that out. Twice.

The first time Bernie just ignored him, but the second time Bernie glared at Mo and declared the osmotic pressure theory was far-fetched and of no concern because LDS rules applied only to beverages. "**NO sacred principles are at hazard, Mo,**" said Bernie. "The doctors and the elders agree that if it's taken from a tablespoon it's either a medicinal or a tonic. Eating fruit is even less like drinking than taking liquid from a spoon."

After scolding Mo, though, Bernie relaxed. Clapping and cheering at the pole dancers' goings-on and takings-off, Bernie shared with the group this was his favorite seat in his favorite office away from the office. Then he added, "Oh, if Della's ever on vacation and one of you guys answers my phone late on a Friday afternoon, tell the caller that Mr. Greenspan has gone to the Polish Ballet."

The crowd was raucous, but Bernie overcame the flood of background noise with a zillion questions about rumors and what was really going on in the offices.

When Bernie excused himself to go to the men's room, Mo and John rose to let Bernie leave the table. John decided he'd best go, too, but he took his second G&T with him and poured all but a bit into the urinal. Three G&Ts would set him on his ass.

Bellied up to the urinal, John noticed a black wingtip like Bernie's beneath the next stall wall. And a navy blue, pinstripe pants cuff. A moment later a little tape recorder clattered onto the floor next to John's shoe. The suit cursed softly as the recorder was retrieved. The curses sounded like Bernie's voice.

John recalled how Bernie held his left arm out on the table during the questioning. Was there a mike in his sleeve?

John fled the men's room but made a wrong turn, so Bernie beat him back to the booth. Mo had slid over into Bernie's corner seat. Bernie was standing by the table, ordering Mo to move, but Mo was laughing. He was keeping the seat because Bernie's raised corner seat had a way better view of the lounge center and the exotic dancer's pole.

Mo, the overweight lightweight computer geek, wouldn't budge. His eyeballs were budging, though—even as he talked to Bernie, Mo and the pole dancer were having a Silicon Valley meets Silicone Mountains moment.

Bernie finally sat where Mo had been. John took his earlier seat, but now seated next to Bernie, John couldn't whisper a warning to the guys about the wire. It came to John that he'd be wise to act a little bit intoxicated so Bernie would think he was hearing naught but *vino veritas* if John found himself having to speak.

A few minutes later, the steaks arrived. The cuts were generous but too chewy and a shade overdone. Bernie was picking up the check, though, so what could they say? John was sure that anything they said could be held against them.

A moment after John cut into his steak, Bernie cut into the beef. If he couldn't watch the pole dancers without twisting his neck and peeking around John's long nose, he could damn well turn to his second love, badgering subordinates about what they should have done.

Glaring again at Mo, Bernie cranked up the flame on the table lamp to its highest setting, pulled a note pad out of his inner suit pocket, and seized the opportunity to take "notes on what you've been doing". Bernie added that he'd finish the performance write-ups in his office, but time was short and he needed "a few basic facts".

Every chance he got, John peeked at Bernie's note pad, but Bernie had dreadful handwriting.

Bernie opened the inquisition by saying that everyone present just might learn something while he and Lawrence discussed the year's activities. It took Bernie seven, maybe eight minutes to filet Lawrence. It wasn't an interview; it was an arraignment. When Bernie stopped, Lawrence was slumped in his seat, with only one bite of his steak eaten and his ever-present smile twisted into a grimace.

Cy was seated next to Lawrence and directly across from John, so John was able to draw Cy's attention to the tiny microphone peeking out from Bernie's cuff. Cy caught the drift and noting the hose job that Bernie laid on Lawrence, braced himself.

Bernie reread his Lawrence notes, ripped off the sheets of paper, and stuffed them into a pocket. He ceremoniously wrote "Cyrus" at the top of a fresh page, but before he started in on Cy, he flipped over three or four pages, and wrote "Maurice" on the top of the sheet. Bernie glared at Mo. Seeing that Mo was engrossed by the pole dancer, Bernie drew a heavy black "X" through "Maurice".

After putting down five Old Fashioneds, Mo was fat, dumb, happy, and blissfully unaware that he'd traded his porthole entry into management for the sake of keeping Bernie's seat with the unobstructed view of the naked ladies.

John was frantic. He'd hoped that Mo would fare so badly that he'd look good by comparison, but now, with Mo crossed off, John's last ray of hope was dashed. John knew that after the screw-up on the thermal fuse project, Bernie would take him over the barrel on the Mark 47 semiconductor board layout. Any number of sins and errors flashed through his mind. Worse still, John feared he'd choke and fall apart when he tried to answer Bernie's first real question. And Bernie would have dozens of real questions. John had no more chance than a pig in a football factory.

A plan congealed in John's mind. He'd fall off his chair at the instant Bernie began his second page of notes on Cy. Grunting, John would grab at his throat as if strangling on the steak. He'd sprawl on the floor, kicking spasmodically.

The chunk of steak was already in John's mouth when IT happens.

The White Knight[19] appears! Blanche! Not in shining armor, mind you, but in waitstaff get-up; a lacy maid's hat, scanties, the minimum[20] legal sheer-to-the-waist panty hose, and little bitty red poinsettia pasties. He'd heard that Blanche had gone back to her roots and was working part-time at a massage parlor and moonlighting at a bar, but instead of moonlighting, here she is, mooning at the El Raunchito.

Blanche announces that she'd spied John from across the room and has traded two of her tables to Edie for this table. She introduces herself as John's former little wifey, but it isn't as if she'd be mistaken for anyone else because damn near all of Blanche is right here on display. John looks her over and supposes that a dermatologist would see more skin. It would be a close call, though.

As she sizes up the tip potentials from the five at the table, Bernie tries to shoo her away. Blanche ignores him because she mistakes Mo for the boss — after all, Mo is the drunkest, he looks older than Bernie, and he's in the commander's seat. Reveling in every minute of John's dread embarrassment and claiming that she wants to get the orders for the next round of drinks exactly right, Blanche leans way, way over the table. She says she wants to be sure to hear every word.

---

[19] White Knight—John's savior is a Blanche night instead of a White Knight. Close enough.
[20] Albuquerque City Ordinance (4/U: No. 69)

Blanche has bad teeth but good cheek bones so if she doesn't smile, she'll have a pretty face even when she's old. On this December evening, though, there are two upfront reasons, one like a wilted rutabaga and the other like a sausage, why she is waiting tables and not up on the stage performing.

It's the Playboy Mansion versus nudist resort thing — the botched Juarez clinic silicone implant in lefty failed so it's longer than righty. Lots longer. Righty droops, but lefty dangles. The difference isn't so obvious when she's standing upright but when she's leaning way over, ho boy.

Trying to be sexy, she sways to make them swing to and fro. Mesmerizing, like pendulums — short righty fast, long lefty slow — tick tock — Tick — tick tock — Tock — tick tock...

As Blanche stretches toward Mo to rerereconfirm his order, her left gazonga hangs perilously close to the chimney of the blazing lamp.

Seeing that Blanche's boob is about to be set afire, John springs into action and snatches the lamp away.

At this moment Bernie springs into action, too. He'd been getting into Cy's face and failings with real dedication when Blanche arrived, but Bernie was not the kind of guy who was about to let two boobs and a pretty face deter him from laying a wood on a subordinate.

Knowing that touching a hand to any part of the waitresses is strictly verboten by the house rules, Bernie grabs a soup spoon, lifts Blanche's left poinsettia out of his line of sight, and resumes his exploration of Cy's many shortcomings.

Blanche has the five men out of the bar and talking to four cops, three bouncers, and two managers within one minute. The only plausible explanation for the cops getting there so fast is a next-door doughnut shop.

They arrest Bernie for disorderly conduct. The other guys are cordoned off, but John gets a cop's ear long enough to say that Bernie was just trying to prevent Blanche from being burned by the table lamp. Bernie hastily agrees that yes, it was just his reflex reaction. The cops release everyone.

Lesson 2.3: Any lie that keeps your boss' name off the police blotter is a good lie.

Bernie immediately swore all to secrecy. "We work for a classified shop, so this is a matter of national security! This could be a blackmail issue, so if you don't hush it up, I'll hush you up. There will be no squealers." Lawrence and Cy nodded. Mo looked nauseous. John felt a little faint.

John was summoned to Bernie's office on Monday morning for his performance interview. Bernie reiterated that the whole Friday fiasco was a matter of national security and John could be subject to penalties of espionage if word leaked out. Bernie skirted around the taping issue, but almost thanked John for steering the cops into thinking it was just an effort to keep Blanche from being burned.

Not only was John not fired, but in the end, he kept his management spot and got a small raise besides. Bernie wasn't quite ready to put John's name into the blank box on the big org chart, though.

Lawrence congratulated John on not being demoted, and Cy said thanks for bringing the wire to his attention.

Mo got evicted from his office and sent back to a desk amongst the peons in the cube farm. His desk had been cleaned out, the janitor had shampooed the office rug and the office repolarization[21] crew summoned before noon.

So it was that John survived that first performance review. And he somehow got through the second, and then the third. Every review was harrowing, though, because Bernie was a confrontation and drama guy who put no stock into accommodation and happy endings.

How Bernie paid the check was never clear. It's cause for wonder about Blanche's tip, as well, for John saw no money exchanged during the police brouhaha. The sure thing was that whatever amount Bernie paid, he finagled a way to get reimbursed by the company. Bernie took care of Bernie.

Amazingly, John's escape was an unintended benefit of Blanche's attempt to embarrass him. See? You just never know who your friends really are.

This is another case when no action is better than action:

John feared there'd be drama.

- He could have walked out the El Ranchito door.
- He could have protested Bernie's actions at the table.
- He could have called in sick that morning.

But he came out of it smelling like a rose.

---

[21] Office repolarization. Nuclear engineers were way out ahead of the curve on office repolarizing. They'd bring in a neutron generator, put tinfoil over all the glass, and let the whole enchilada bake for a couple hours. Nowadays you'd have to hire two women with stark hairdos and a little gay guy with a Fu Manchu mustache to rework the feng shui.

Chapter 3

Writing Performance Reviews

Doing performance reviews with good performing subordinates isn't easy and must be done well, but is typically straightforward. Apart from angst attributable to HR constraints imposing bell curve distributions of evaluations, forced rankings, and the like, that is.

The reviews for the employees needing correction are more difficult, but if the review process does indeed set even one employee onto a path to better performance, the manager will find this effort a satisfying and rewarding investment.

The contentious reviews are for the employees who are on the verge of termination. Thankfully, these situations are rare, but if handled poorly, the consequences can be dreadful. The manager must be far more careful with pre-termination reviews. This chapter is directed toward these unpleasant and effort-intensive situations.

Personnel actions to terminate poorly performing employees usually involve exhuming prior performance reviews. The uninitiated might imagine these reviews to be smoking-gun evidence of continued substandard work, but all too often these smoking guns miss the reviewee and shoot a hole in the reviewer's foot.

Case Study

Our man John set out to terminate his subordinate Stuart Pidder on the grounds of well-documented flagrant nonfeasance and egregious malfeasance.

However, when Stu's previous performance review was disinterred, Human Resources (HR) found that amidst the mound of negative evidence, John had written the terms "...acceptable job..." and "...competent...".

John's terms "...acceptable job..." and "...competent..." were clothed to the armpits in caveats. Well, up to the crotch, anyway. His exact words were, "Only when given the benefit of every doubt could it be said that Pidder was doing a marginally acceptable job at a single simple task." Further, "To perform this single task, Pidder needed to be no more competent than could be reasonably expected of an illiterate, minimum wage worker whose brain function was unsullied by training."

Unfortunately, John's contexts, caveats, and smart-ass remarks were laundered away during the mandatory pre-termination HR versus terminating supervisor browbeating session. "Performance reviews **must** strike an encouraging tone," HR said. Trumpeting the words "acceptable" and "competent", the host of negatives in Stu's performance review were turned to toast. Thus, it became John, not Stu, who needed the asbestos boxers.

Instead of John having written and signed proof that Stu was not doing a speck more than diddly and was diddling in a less than condonable manner at that, HR almost induced Stu to think that he was performing in an acceptable, competent manner.

In HR's opinion, based on the performance review document in hand, DA could not terminate Stu without precipitating a sure-to-lose lawsuit.

Lesson 3.1: You can't depend on others playing fair just because you play fair.

Remark: Even if you intend to write only negatives, it's hard to avoid having your words taken out of context. This is particularly a problem if you strive to be fair and ethical by presenting both sides of an argument.

HR did allow John to put the slacker on probationary status for six months, though. During the probationary period, John observed and documented that Stu's work output dwindled and his performance of the dwindled output deteriorated.

What's on John's to do list?

With the end of the probationary status period fast approaching, John needs to revisit the flawed review document and to mend the review process. Doubtlessly, most of the document is correct and can be recycled as the starting point for writing the new review.

To fix the review process, John needs to ensure that his management is on board the Termination Express. A serious meeting with Bernie and Bernie's leader is a must, because without their support the termination effort is futile.

It wouldn't hurt if Bernie explained things to the Corporate Head, Worldwide Department of Resources and Human Development in terms that even he, the CHWDRHD, could understand.

The next step is to repel HR's appeal to retain and retrain Stu for another task. Stu will help John on this:

Stu's case is just another teaching-a-boar-hog-to-sing-high-opera problem; it's difficult, the results are poor, and it annoys the hog. Further, this boar hog is a truculent son of a bitch who'd fight over a burnt match, so John can bank on Stu losing his temper in his first HR retention interview.

To assess the company's hopes that retraining Stu would yield benefits, consider that HR and even Stu himself would agree that Stu is not a towering intellect. However, John claiming in the first review that "Stu's dumb as a bucket of hair" might be overstating the case. It takes solid supporting data to make the bucket of hair claim stick. Far better to go with the tried and proven "He's dumb as a sack of hammers". No successful manager allows exaggeration to erode credibility.

John's collection of citation-worthy negatives from the probationary period is impressive. To wit: Pidder's signal contribution to office activities during the probation period was plugging the toilet in the farthest stall in the second-floor men's room on four consecutive days in July **and again** in the first week in August. (The previous record was held by the long-departed Oscar M. — he'd done three consecutive days, but on just the one occasion. Besides, that was way back in '59 when the truckers' strike interrupted the supply of Army surplus toilet paper and Nekoosa paper towels were substituted.)

John's noting of this accomplishment by Stu and detailing why it was so exceptional was appropriate. However, John overshot the bounds of conventional wisdom by adding the comment, "In view of Mr. Pidder's demonstrations of his primary skill, Mr. Pidder's one and only completely appropriate decision during the probationary period was to keep a toilet plunger available at all times. "

However true this might be, there is no place for this level of speculation in a performance review destined for filing in an employee's permanent records.

With the issues above resolved, John is ready to draft a new review covering Pidder's probation. Here's where the tough sledding begins. The three major challenges are:

1. While utilizing content that's utterly devoid of positives, John is faced with writing a review that "strikes a positive note" in the eyes of the HR twinkies.

2. Although praying to both St. Roche[22] and St. Vic could render the termination process essentially irreversible the instant Pidder steps into the HR Terminatetorium Chamber, HR will want to cover their ass (CTA) by forcing the review to include a clause providing a pathway for escape from probationary status.

3. Concurrently, John's management ladder needs to be hornswoggled into thinking they understand the performance review and thus induced to sign off on the document.

---

[22] HR and Personnel have no assigned Patron Saint (PS), so it's between St. Roche, the PS of Dogs, Plagues, and Pestilence, and St. Victor of Marseilles, the PS of Torture Victims.

John's task is to thread the needle, with text meeting the HR criteria and yet sufficiently vague that no statement in the review is taken out of context and used to declare that Stu was an adequate or even marginally acceptable performer.

So, what are John's options?

John has only one option. He must master obfuscation and weasel wording. Quality weaseling goes far beyond merely making conditional or qualified statements; it goes all the way to skillfully creating precision holistic ambiguity.

Regrettably, a long-standing shortfall in management training is the absence of tutelage in the arts and skills of obfuscation and weasel wording.

Newspaper reporters weasel all the time. Their use of "alleged" to describe crime situations is almost universal.

Example: "The alleged victim was found lying nude in a pool of blood at the foot of the stairs, her neck almost severed between the 4th and 5th vertebrae, her once-beautiful lingerie model's body allegedly totally exsanguinated, and the blade of a stainless steel hand ax buried in the back of her skull. Foul play is allegedly alleged. "

Marketing and ad men are also expert weaselers. The proof is just comparing the bold print with the fine print. Lawyers are leaders in the field. Politicians build whole careers and even nations with weaseling.

Unlike advertisers, lawyers, and politicians, John is in R&D management, where managers are trained to obtusely answer questions by stating fact. Poor John is naïve and utterly without coaching in weaseling or obfuscation.

John desperately needs a tool if not for weaseling, then certainly for obfuscation; in his shop and throughout the land employee terminations are rare, but the costs of tied hands when termination is necessary are large and growing.

Lesson 3.2: Presenting a balanced argument that can't be misconstrued is so difficult that creative obfuscation is our only practical solution.

Exhibit 1

A Personnel Buzz Phrase Generator

Weasel wording is a topic-specific skill with formal training available only in journalism and in law schools, but excellent tools for obfuscatory wording are widely available to commoners in the technological fields. Technospeak Buzz Phrase Generators have been around for 50 or more years and now may be easily accessed with Google. These new Google-accessed generators are wondrous things—you enter the desired numbers of modifiers and out pops a buzz phrase of the required length.

The old hard-copy 10-row x 3-column adverb-adjective-noun phrase generators provide an understanding of how the generators work, however. With these generators, you select a random 3-digit number, say 429. The 4th entry in column 1 is Adaptively. The 2nd entry in column 2 is Systematized. The 9th entry in column 3 is Processing. Voila! Adaptively Systematized Processing! It sounds just as if it means something! From this little table, you have instant access to 1000 lovely sounding phrases that are utterly disconnected from fact.

Even beyond **Dilbert** cartoons, these generated phrases have proven to be useful things. Unfortunately, though, when Technospeak buzz phrases are overutilized at professional meetings or other public forums, some know-it-all in the audience will understand. He'll rise to take issue and face is lost.

Since Technospeak buzzies don't travel well and totally fail in personnel applications, John and the world of management are crying out for a buzz phrase generator for performance reviews. Would it be possible to create a generator? Certainly! There will surely be a place for three column buzz phrases. Moreover, we are in luck for several reasons:

1. Personnel concerns are more fertile ground for fog shoveling than the hopelessly factual techie scene.

2. Chances are that any personnel buzz phrase will look good and have a lovely bouquet. Personnel assessment terminology is inherently fuzzy-winky-touchy-feely, so if you can cite even one credible scenario where your buzz phrase is apparently relevant, it will be nigh impossible for senior management and/or HR to dismiss your phrase out of hand. And should you somehow fail to conjure up a thread of relevance for your first creation, you can always find another three-digit random number — you have 1000 ways to score.

3. It is highly likely that the personnel evaluation will be read by only a few and scrutinized by none but you. The odds are very good that no reader other than you will bother to look up a word while reading the review.

4. Finally, dare we say, your bioequivalent of Stu Pidder will be no more compulsive about his reading of the performance review than with his work assignments. He will be eager and foolish enough to believe that your avalanche of obfuscation is a positive assessment.

The personnel terminology buzz phrase generator

Our buzz phrase generator contains three elements:

First: A column of ten soaring, exulting, and utterly superficial adverbs.

Second: A column of ten adjectives that sound happy and proclaim nothing.

Third: A column of ten nouns. You are free to choose your set of nouns; they should somehow seem to relate, in a slippery way, to the employee's status, function, or degree of dysfunction. The important thing is that none of the adverbs, adjectives, or nouns explicitly state a value, either positive or negative.

The adverbs

There are several reasons why Southern debutantes are sent to finishing school. The basics are instruction in manners, style, poise, grace, and training in the arts. More importantly, though, the young ladies are instructed in the fine art of genteel, intelligent debate. That is, they are coached to express doubt by saying "Incredible!" instead of "Bullshit!" We exploit this phenomenon with our first column, the adverbs.

0. Incredibly—The word sounds incredibly good, but it exactly means not credible. How could it be more incredible?

1. Staggeringly—Staggeringly is such a fine word! So many elusive mental images.

2. Stunningly—This word sounds like text from *People* magazine. It could be positive. On the other hand, it could be so bad that it causes stupefying paralysis.

3. Inexplicably—Maybe even more incredible than incredible. It's a disconnect between facts and appearances, and happily, the disconnect vanishes in the absence of thought.

4. Dazzlingly—Dazzling means glittering. Just as all that glitters is not gold, all that dazzles is not fact.

5. Uniquely—this means matchlessly or inimitably. None the same? It could be that there being no more than one of him makes the world a better place.

6. Fantastically—Most readers think of fantastically good when they see the word fantastically. And that's the fantasy.

7. Uncompromisingly—Compromise has evolved, becoming a soiled word. Thus, uncompromising must now be an unsoiled word. But uncompromising just means inflexible—he does not give in, give up, or listen to reason.

8. Unquantifiably—Defies quantification. But why? Is it too wondrous to place a number upon it? Is it so ephemeral as to defy grasping? Or is it so tiny that it can scarcely be seen, let alone measured?

9. Absolutely—Most assuredly. Totally and definitely; without question. But the word doesn't offer any evaluation, so whatever it is, it sure as hell is that.

An alternative adverb to consider is unbelievably.

The punctuation option

An additional optional feature could be added after the adverb. Astutely inserting a comma, a semicolon, a dash, or a series of several periods after the adverb could easily create a significant amplification of the ambiguity overload.

Caution is needed here, however, for we have observed that periods tend to break the surface tension and cause the reader to start thinking about what he has just read. We certainly don't want to prompt the reader to think. Avoid colons as well, for they have the same or even a more negative impact than periods.

In some cases, the punctuation mark will make no sense at all, but in other cases punctuation following the adverb totally warps the statement's interpretation and finely controlled warpage is almost always a major enhancement.

The adjectives

Next, we will need ten adjectives. The reviewee needs to leave the interview believing the review was flattering. Hence, the statements must sound superficially encouraging. It is critical to avoid frightening the review victim, for he might repent. You can't allow him to reform before you have the separation papers signed, his ID badge in your hand, and you've got him out beyond the guard gate. Remember this — reformation will not make a hopelessly incompetent guy competent, but it will look good to HR and force you to start all over. This show ain't over 'til the fat lady sings, folks.

So, for personnel evaluations, these words need to sound happy or somehow be positive in and of themselves but must hold minimal meaning out of context and are sufficiently vague to impede assessment. Desirable adjectives have non-positive synonyms and are usually expected to be heard in a positive context.

We must **at all costs** avoid terms that are used, or are equivalent to those used, in the HR scoring for your Stu Pidder's performance. Do not repeat John's mistake and use "competent" or "acceptable" in any context. We can't allow terms alleging Good, Better, and Best to creep in.

Some possible adjectives:

0. Optimistic—Optimism is such a happy thing. And groundless optimism in the face of negative fact is such a keen indicator of lack of understanding.

1. Spontaneous—Perhaps this is most superficial of all superficial characteristics. Irish setters are spontaneous and happy, and they are the dumbest of all sporting dogs. Unending spontaneity indicates a lack of focus or planning.

2. Decisive—Decisiveness is a good thing. Unless the decisions are bad. And then it's a really bad thing. Bull-headed is an appropriate synonym for decisive.

3. Marvelous—This is a fan mail text word. Superficially it sounds ultra-positive, but it only means that it causes one to marvel. The eye roll is optional.

4. Unconventional—This could mean anything from innovative to loose cannon. It suggests that work style, strategies, or solutions are unlikely to conform. Your Stu is more likely to take it as a positive if you mildly disvalue conformity in your oral (and duly non-recorded) comments as you go through the review document with him.

5. Omnidirectional—It sounds powerful and impressive, but it means on any random vector. Up, down, left, right, all around—hence forward, backward, or turvy topsy.

6. Exciting—Exciting is usually taken to indicate a positive emotion, but negatives can be equally exciting. Panic is very exciting. Terror is mess-the-pants exciting.

7. Surreal — The word sounds like it might mean super real, but it actually means anything except real. It's weird, odd, unreal, dreamlike, bizarre, or characterized by fantastic imagery or incongruous juxtapositions.

8. Meretricious — This is a word for all needs. It can mean plausible, persuasive, tawdry, flashy, or specious. Most who hear the word mistake it for having something to do with merit.

9. Deliberate — This could mean thoughtful, or it could mean plodding.

A utility alternative for an adjective above is Impressive. Impressive could mean imposing, striking, extraordinary, or notable, but it does not carry a value judgment. Another fine alternative is fabulous — it arises from fable. A third is solid. Dense things are solids. Unbelievable could be used here if unbelievably is not selected as an adverb.

The adjectives could be enhanced by punctuation marks, as was suggested for the adverbs. Randomly inserting commas will confuse the casual reader but carries the hazard of prompting the skimmer to read more carefully. Hence, readers must be well vetted if punctuation enhancement is utilized.

The nouns

There is need for ten essentially vague nouns to label the review victims. In order to create text customized for a specific application, it will be appropriate to vary the noun column entries toward the niche of the target worker, the persona, or the lack thereof. Here are some ideas to consider:

Characterizations by the role the employee plays

This is intended to convey, in informal terms, the niche the employee occupies in the organization:

0. Rock—This might be a dependable person who can always be counted upon, or maybe this worker is more like a heavy, inert chunk of mineral aggregate that sinks right to the bottom in almost any fluid environment.

1. Anchor—This worker could be the lead spokesperson or a dependable asset. Anchors are also devices that prevent your ship from moving until hoisted out of their secure position.

2. Heavyweight vs heavy weight—Here we have a key person who asserts a presence in his field, or we have a weighty encumbrance. If there is a half space key on your keyboard, this is the place to use it. Either that or mess with the kerning.

3. Bulwark—Bulwarks are fortifications. Or barriers.

4. Concrete addition—This could be a worker who brings solid and substantial skills and work to the organization, for the word 'concrete' means solid and substantial. But do consider that concrete is a mixture of finely ground baked limestone, rocks, and water. It starts as a fluid, but once hardened, it never changes again and does doing nothing but take up space.

5. Jump-starter—This phrase was borrowed from auto applications to refer to an individual who brings previously amassed energy into a new application and thus rapidly and forcefully starts this new application. On the other hand, it could be referring to someone who can't get started without a jump of outside energy. Output or input is the issue here.

6. Bastion—A bastion can be a mainstay or stronghold but it's more likely the last place an out-of-date idea is held.

7. Keystone—This guy could be a rock that holds everything in order, or he just prevents movement. Keystones are just wedges pinned in cracks between two other rocks. A wedge works as a two-direction lever, so it's a two-way simple tool.

8. No-brainer—It could be that this guy is so good that anybody can see it without thinking. Or, it may be that this guy operates without brain function.

9. Outside-the-boxers—Management lauds and prizes innovators who think up unconventional, outside-the-box solutions. Society is less generous toward individuals who do their best work when outside their boxers.

The worker's role generator:

Here's the generator for the worker's roles case:

0	Incredibly	Optimistic	Rock
1	Staggeringly	Spontaneous	Anchor
2	Stunningly	Decisive	Heavy weight
3	Inexplicably	Marvelous	Bulwark
4	Dazzlingly	Unconventional	Concrete addition
5	Uniquely	Omnidirectional	Jump-starter
6	Fantastically	Exciting	Bastion
7	Uncompromisingly	Surreal	Keystone
8	Unquantifiably	Meretricious	No-brainer
9	Absolutely	Deliberate	Outside-the-boxers

The new employee in deep doo-doo:

Assuming your intent is to give a relatively new employee a ticket on another bus, here are some status words for the least to most threatened newbie worker. We might incite bad press with actions to immolate our young. So, we must be gentle in our judgment scale of employee value until the useless child is well out the door. Accordingly, these terms do not materially enhance phasic ambiguity.

These terms are: Junior associate, trainee, neophyte, nominal, unproven, quasi-temporary, provisional, forewarned, on-warning, and probationary. To complete phrases to achieve contextual sense, it may be helpful to attach a non-added value term such as 'worker', 'employee under review', 'person', 'personage' or 'subject' to the terms in the third column. Note here that 'personage' is usually taken to infer the person is a VIP or celebrity, but it may also indicate the person does not merit identification.

The experienced worker's persona situation:

In the case of the retired-in-place worker, the persona and work avoidance strategy of the worker will be well known. Hence, the spectrum here is directed toward taking initiative, taking risks, and seeking adventure.

Risk varies from ultra-high (he dares tell his wife that she does indeed look fat in her new outfit), to not quite so eager to take chances and acting like a bullet-proof special op mercenary, to the ultra-low hapless alopecia pygiata[23] victim. Since you have the worker's persona already in hand, you may wish to trichotomize the noun column into three categories that focus on the worker, such as "Risk seeker", "Risk acceptor" and "Risk avoider". You would then have only 300 phrases from which to choose, but most will sound like they are appropriate.

Here are the full set of risk-based labels:

Fat wife critic, special ops guy, winger, risk seeker, risk acceptor, risk manager, performer, Obsessive Compulsive Disorder hyper-planner, alopecia pygiata case.

Terms for the guy who takes up space:

This final set of terms is intended to describe space occupants. Here the goal is to utilize a neutral term that portrays the guy who shows up for work and collects a paycheck. He is part of the operation, warms a chair and consumes oxygen, but is nothing, does nothing, and contributes nothing of worth. The guy is a cipher, but cipher is too precisely defined as meaning a nobody; you must not label anyone a cipher until after he is out the door.

---

[23] Alopecia pygiata—The less-rare-than-commonly thought masculine affliction of not having a hair on his ass.

Some possible terms are: Teammate, participant, role player, member, colleague, associate, partaker, accomplice, follower, adherent, secondary, accessory. Although these terms are relatively neutral, they fail to enhance ambiguity. You can likely develop a list that better fits your specific needs.

Social use of phrase generator

These generators could be easily adapted for use in a smart phone or similar device. This would access to the buzz phrases at cocktail parties, while you are walking the dog, strolling up to the microphone at a professional meeting amid thunderous applause, or in any social situation when you wish to totally snow your friends and acquaintances.

Summary

Let's restate the plan. The goal is to write the performance review in such a way that clarity exists only in an ephemeral way. The words glitter and glow, passing though the mind of the beholder in warm and fuzzy ways. For our purposes, the more possible interpretations, the better. At the end of the day, if several readers agree upon the meanings of your review statements, you have failed in your task—unless, of course, their sandals all tread down the same primrose path.

Chapter 4

Rumor Management

The management training gurus' mantra is that miscommunication is the bane of management and rumors are the worst of all miscommunications.

It's our sacred duty, they declare, to take up their crusade to stamp out rumors, once and for all! Gee! The power brokers all seem to agree about this, so it must be a swell idea. We suppose.

But just how do we stamp out rumors? The gurus say if we just always speak truths, rumors will vanish as the morning mists. We have not found this to be universally true.

- Rumors are hard to discredit because they contest the official management line and when the conflict is acute, the rumor has as good a shot at being true as the front office attempts to oil the troubled waters.

- A rumor is usually on-the-spot timely because it connects what's happening this week to what the troops have heard happened last week.

- Rumors are understood because they are in the language of the workplace, not manager-speak.

- If we knock down a rumor here, it just pops up over there in a slightly different form.

- Rumor mongers often claim to report *the real reasons* why things are as they are. Our official statements make mealy-mouthed comments on whats but rarely mention whys.

- Rumors shamelessly pander to homo sapien's base emotions and anything done in a shameless manner will be attractive.

- When a truly outrageous rumor catches fire, all we can achieve is damage control. Our only option is coexistence.
- There is an endless supply of rumors. These days they hide between the pages of Facebook and ooze into every workplace through the voids between management's decrees.

It's time to face facts. The only inevitable things in life are death, taxes, and rumors. Since we cannot stamp out rumors no matter how hard we try, why don't we go from futilely attempting to manage rumors to management by rumors?

Management by rumor

Suppose you have a management plan. It's "Your Plan". Imagine anonymously floating a rumor about Your Plan past every critical eye in the department. The real workers might note a few benefits while the naysayers and drones will espy and denounce every flaw in Your Plan. They will protest every pain and suffering it could possibly cause. For your purposes, the big benefits will be seen as flaws by the non-producers.

Now, if you could just tap into these critiques, you'd have all the knowledge needed to tailor Your Plan in the precise manner to maximize the benefits. Or pains. Or even hit that sweet spot of shade for the many and sunshine for you. Indeed, for the cunning manager willing to invest careful thought and effort, management by rumor has real promise.

Let's think about floating a rumor to achieve a management goal. What will you need in the rumor? This might be a little tricky, because you'll need a rumor that advances Your Plan, properly integrates the workers' bleak thoughts, and isn't perceived as your idea in any way at all. Remember, too, that the staff will tend to push back at anything that seems like it might favor management

First, you'll need **motivation** for starting a rumor. You could start the rumor to:

i)   Enable the candid, but likely biased, generation of opinions about Your Plan.
ii) Mobilize opposition to Your Plan.
iii) Advance the cause of Your Plan
iv) Handicap the opposition to Your Plan.
v)   Settle a score with an individual enemy or competitor via Your Plan.
vi) Sow discord among the troops.

Second, you will need a plan to **utilize the knowledge** and contingency plans in case things go awry. These will depend on the purpose of the rumor.

i)   Plan A—what you'll do with the knowledge you hope to gain
ii) Plans B1, B2,...Bn—contingency plans for situations when the rumor misses its mark
iii) Plan C—plan for evacuation of Dodge if things go to hell in a handbasket

Third, rumor content may vary widely, but your rumor must not over-promise. Unfulfilled expectations rather than hardships per se are the usual source of serious angers, so regardless of whether all, part, or none of the synthetic rumor comes true, the synthetic rumor should predict no more than a minimally positive net effect for the staff.

As an example of the hazards of over-promising, suppose that for many years this dude in Minnesota has been getting along just fine by keeping his little wifey pregnant all summer and barefoot all winter. But then just to tease her, he arranges for her to hear the rumor that he's going to get her fur booties and have her tubes tied. Well, if he then shows up with a pair of flip-flops from K-Mart and tells her that he's feeling horny, she's gonna **kill** the son of a bitch.

Fourth, you must have a way to **control** rumor **content**, particularly after the rumor goes viral. Downstream content control is difficult because rumors are evolving organisms.

    i)   Make sure that the rumor as sown is what you want.

    ii)   Do everything you can to ensure that those with the power to squelch your rumor won't do so before the rumor gets entrenched. The ideal situation is when a powerful party with a dog in the fight seizes upon your rumor as advantageous to them. They will likely take up the rumor's cause, preserving and advancing it.

    iii)   Robust rumors contain enough fact to be credible and yet have sufficient ambiguity to resist quick repudiation.

Fifth, the rumor needs to be **seeded** in fertile soil. You need to get the rumor onto the tongues of the community opinion leaders without them knowing the rumor is aimed at advancing Your Plan. Some seeding ideas are:

    i)   A weakly sealed CONFIDENTIAL envelope left poorly hidden on your desk. Use a generic envelope so the snooper thinks he can tear the envelope open, read/copy the contents, and replace the whole envelope without being detected. The contents should mildly denounce Your Plan, citing the obvious flaws.

ii)   Mild fault finding re Your Plan on a poorly erased chalk board, with trash basket supplements.

iii)   Do a night out with the boys for group-wise *vino veritas*. This is not easy to do well. See **The Sting** — Henry knew how to do this.

iv)   Using an associate to do the seeding is usually poor and directing a subordinate to seed the rumor for you is hopeless.

Sixth, a way to **assess reaction to the rumor** is required. You will need to collect data, but you can't afford to be seen as actively seeking out information.

i)   Listen passively to both what is said and who said it, and keep records of these facts.

ii)   Good news is not credible unless verified. Bad news is inherently credible.

iii)   Do mix with the troops at coffee and lunch, listening, and when forced to voice your ideas, offer few positive opinions. Mildly negative opinions that focus on well-known shortfalls of Your Plan should be okay — you won't be telling them anything they don't already know and you'll seem to be at most non-committal toward Your Plan. Do make it seem as if you care about their concerns, particularly if you do not.

iv)   You will want to hear the strong negative opinions because the strong negatives are usually driven by alpha guys with little workplace empires. Empire erosion is usually a positive thing.

Seventh, you will need **rumor support**

    i)   We know that there is always a little truth in every good lie. But should the rumor's core claim be rank fantasy, you will need a way to embellish it with factual details that lend credence. Creation of factoid details to support rumors is a trainable skill.

    ii)   Arranging a surreptitious meeting is a good way to get the troops to think something is afoot. Unnamed auxiliary guests at these meetings are a nice extra, and if you can manage to cajole an in-house lawyer and an HR rep into attending, you'll even have some attendees suspecting that something big is coming down. Make sure all attendees wear clean neckties and carry nice briefcases. No crappy shoes, either, unless you are trying to sell an unknown visitor as a government regulatory slug.

Eighth, rumor follow-up is a must. And keep in mind that there may be fallout from just circulating the rumor, even if no part of the rumored action ever comes to pass.

    i)   There may be both winners and losers. People might leave, but just make the best of it. If the prospect of working under the new circumstance is seen to be so grim that Long Ben Slackdoff threatens to retire and open a bait shop, tell him you'll drop by because you're looking for a new reel. Ask him what's biting, too.

ii)   Ben's departure will be addition by subtraction, but keep in mind that the prospect of a new order of things could drive your number one rising star out the door, too.

One final comment—pushback at management makes management's vigorous rumor repudiations serve to validate rather than quell rumors.

Case Study: Cy's 401k/PAC rumor

John lacked adequate *cojones* for synthesizing rumors, but every few months Bernie ran a trial banner up the flagpole to see who saluted and which fingers they displayed while saluting. The other managers took Bernie's trials as sanction and implied permission for such mischief, so the bald and cunning Cy was forever manipulating true lies. One of his was a doozy.

When he heard about the newly legislated 401k savings plans, Cy's first reaction was that there just had to be something special in it for him. He immediately began a search for a 401k ploy that would enable him to piggy-back on his fellow workers' deposits in order to achieve one or more of his four career go-to goals:

Good—To line his pockets

Better—To gain fame and stuff his pockets

Better Still—To advance his career and fill his pockets

Best—To lay waste and ruin to the career aspirations of one or more competitors

Cy soon found the 401k rules were too tight, though. He could find no keyhole.

Remark: This might have been Cy's luckiest ever failure. Violating 401k law is a serious offense, the chances of getting caught are high, the prosecution is unrelenting, and the penalties are premium grade ass-in-sling events.

Cy remained convinced, though, that if lots of money changed hands, a smart guy could find a way to get a cut of the action. So, he invented a rumor — that the company was considering starting 100% matching support for 401k deposits, but only via ultra-confidential invitations extended to a top-secret list of selected employees.

The wrinkle that set this rumor apart from all the rest was that the invitation criterion wasn't going to be a rank-has-its-privileges thing; it was going to be a litmus test for company loyalty. This was a big deal right at the time because the company was lobbying for a huge local taxation easement. These tax advantages were to be granted ONLY IF the right politicians won in the upcoming election. Hence, contributing to the correct election coffers was sure to be seen in the halls of deep carpets as an unquestionably laudable and quantifiable loyalty act.

Those who were willing to stand up and pony down a threshold or better sum to the grand-sounding Desert Aromatics Political Action Committee (DAPAC) would clearly be the most loyal employees.

According to Cy's plan, all the DAPAC donation money would be funneled into an account controlled by the troika of Cy and two of his long-term cronies.

Surely, Cy thought, significant political favors for the troika members would accrue. Further, even if the anticipated political plums fell short of expectations, the DAPAC disbursements could easily be attenuated. This would ensure that he and his buddies would have access to a fine little floating slush fund.

At a meeting with the higher ups, Cy presented the DAPAC plan. Enthusiasm reigned. By acclamation Cy was named to chair the DAPAC.

The Big Boys had two significant changes in the plan; the PAC had to be of the non-connected type, and renamed the Grass Roots Political Action Committee (GRPAC). This would create the illusion that the PAC was driven by the workers and not by the company. Perception being nine points of the law, the Big Boys wanted it to look like the PAC was utterly independent of Desert Aromatics. It was to be just coincidence that all the contributors worked at Desert Aromatics.

When someone hinted that it smelled a bit disingenuous, the Big Boys suggested that it would be good if the employees whose wives did not go by their husband's surnames would declare their contributions under the wives' names.

Upon the Big Boys' approval, Cy duly circulated the announcement of the formation of GRPAC. The Big Boys were ecstatic; company loyalty was flourishing, they claimed, because these three guys formed GRPAC in and of their own volition. The GRPAC trio were deemed by one and all to be truly company men.

Lesson 4.1: It's easy to believe that Desert Aromatics wanted the tax breaks and even easier to believe that the DA Big Boys would fully expect to reap favors from PAC contributions.

Remark: Knowing the usual level of hypocrisy in the headquarters building, it's totally easy to believe that the company would like the world to think it was only the named PAC contributors and not the company pressing for the election of the chosen slate of candidates.

With GRPAC established, Cy implemented his little gem rumor. There were two choke points; there must be no smoking gun paper trail connecting the PAC and 401ks, and the rumor had to appear to come from on high.

So, on the Sunday afternoon before Labor Day, he slipped into the deep-carpet conference room in the headquarters building. He carried a bag of crumpled notes seeming to relate to the upcoming election vis-à-vis the PAC and loyalty, and another bag of crumpled and ripped papers with ideas about 401k plans. None of the notes bore names or dates. He used multiple colored pens and markers and all grades of different handwriting on the notes.

When he left, the chalkboard was in a raggedly erased state and the trash baskets filled with notes about company loyalty and other notes about possible 401k plans and incentives. He made very sure that no scrap of paper had both PAC and 401k/incentives written thereon.

He was smart, too, by doing it on Sunday before the Monday holiday. The janitors would be sure to leave lots of their routine Friday cleaning chores undone so they'd have to come in Monday to collect their double-time holiday pay for doing what they should have done on Friday for regular time pay. Further, since it was a holiday, they'd have no supervisory oversight and lots of time to read, poke in the trash baskets, and converse while doing their cleanup work.

The chalkboard and trash basket ploy worked like a charm. The janitor carefully recorded every letter, dash, and squiggle of what he thought he deciphered on the chalkboard. Then he called in the other janitor and together they examined the chalkboard for a half-hour or more before they rigorously cleaned it. They scooped up the 401k notes and the trashed PAC/company loyalty litmus test notes. After they and another buddy studied the notes that evening, the expected conclusions were drawn.

The word was out across the lower echelons of the company by noon on Tuesday. Even the minor managers had heard the rumor by noon Wednesday, and they, more than any other strata of employees, knew proof by checkbook trumps proof by pudding every time. There was close to $10k in the pot by the end of that first week.

The Big Boys soon learned of the rumor about 401k contribution matches, but since they enjoyed the concept of GRPAC purchases of political power favors and since the 401k matching issue had never been on their table, they felt no pressing need to slow the donations by publicly declaring that the 401k matching issue was a myth.

When a reporter asked, "Is the company rewarding employees for contributing to a PAC?" the official response was as expected; "Oh, we wouldn't do that kind of thing! That might be seen as unethical. "

Lesson 4.2: The notion that a plan is a bit subversive lends great credibility to rumors.

Unfortunately for Cy, the Feds uncovered a PAC-slush fund scheme in Amarillo just as the GRPAC's donations really got rolling. The threat of examiners forced Cy to set aside his plans for his very own purchased political favors — the only favors that the now-wary politicos would dare promise were steps to affect work rules and the squeakiest clean tax breaks. The Big Boys ordered GRPAC to ensure their accounting and disbursement procedures were airtight. With the hope for political favors lost and the slush fund idea on life support, Cy had gained naught.

Cy was undeterred. The donation flow was dwindling, but Cy had friends in low places. Citing rising bookkeeping expenses to his fellow GRPAC troikans, Cy negotiated a deal with a "survey research" company. In fact, the survey research was just a front for an operation that sold, to the highest bidder, donors' phone numbers, together with a range of identifiers. The survey research company negotiated an agreement with a telemarketer. Cy got 50% of the proceeds. He was less than utterly candid with his brother troikans in issues regarding the kickback.

As could be expected, the government examiners heard the rumor linking the 401k plan with the PAC donations and came calling. Since no official company communication ever mentioned any aspect of any 401k plan, the Big Boys were able to deny everything except hearing that some employees had formed a non-connected PAC.

The examiners admitted that they had no case. The Big Boys closed down GRPAC right after the election, anyway, but that was more likely a result of none of their slate of candidates being elected than of examiner pressures. No mention was made that "not quite all" of the GRPAC funds made it into the candidates' coffers before the election.

In late November, one of the Big Boys called Cy in "for a chat." A pro-rata refund of all the funds, that is, "every goddamn red cent!" left in the war chest was suggested. As a result, all the senior management contributors got their pro-rata refunds. Amazingly, during the process of sharing the donor identification files with the survey researchers, the file containing the identifiers for junior management and non-managerial donors had been irreparably corrupted.

It all worked out nicely for Cy. He regretted failing to destroy any competitors' careers, but he won on three of his four goals; he netted about $1k from the kickbacks and when the dust cleared, he and his GRPAC cronies ended up in control of a $13k slush fund. Better still, he amassed kudos in the headquarters building for forming and chairing the PAC.

Lesson 4.3: Large sums can be diverted only when large sums change hands.

Chapter 5

Doing Favors for the Boss

We realists understand that if we accept a gift, we incur a debt. With debts come collection times. Regardless of our convenience regarding time, place, or circumstance, our time to pay up will come. There might be such on Mars or Venus, but on Planet Earth there is no free lunch.

But did you stop to think that giving a needy guy lunch makes it more, not less, likely that you'll be shamed into giving the next needy guy lunch, too? So, you can't give a free lunch, either? Politicians grasp this concept. They like donations, but they LUST for investors. The politicos throw bones to the voters but put their best efforts into finding enthusiasts, for enthusiasts are willing to invest money, effort, and time in a cause or candidate. Investing in a campaign instills a sense of obligation far beyond that created by receiving a few goodies. This is how charities work, too. They want your money but they really want a whole lot more. They want you on their team.

So how does this play out in the work environment? It's easy to imagine that doing a favor for your boss is a good move, particularly if the favor the boss asks of you is difficult, carries a high profile, and the only compensation is his thanks. You leave the boss' office thinking he owes you.

But your boss doesn't owe you; he's just one step closer to owning you. Doing favors for the boss gets you vacuumed into allegiance and the next thing you know you are sharing in the perks that come with being one of his boys. And perks always come with prices.

Case Study

On a Monday afternoon, Bernie told John of a need for an unmarried professional level guy for a "Top Secret" trip to Salt Lake on Friday. Bernie added that it had to be a single guy because it wasn't right to ask a married guy to travel on weekends.

John supposed that his guy Jerome was unmarried because he didn't talk about a wife or kids at coffee break, didn't wear a ring, and John's admin thought Jerome was shy but kind of cute. Although Jerome was a security-cleared BS&P geek, he looked normal enough that he wouldn't stand out in a crowd. John reasoned that meant Jerome was okay for the classified errand and recommended Jerome to Bernie.

Bernie asked if Jerome was upstanding, God-fearing, and sober, these being kosher questions in that era. John said that Jerome was not known as a drinker and had cleared every security check. So, regarding national secrets, John opined, Jerome could be trusted outside the fence.

Remark: So far, John has earned a B-. He's done okay, but misread Bernie's motives. Just as Bernie planned it.

Bernie had just negotiated a contract for Dugway support, and the favor was a courier trip to the Dugway Proving Grounds. Jerome was flattered to be asked, so he told Bernie, "Sure, I'll go to Dugway," without a moment's thought.

Jerome already knew better than to ask for details about Dugway. The DA guys who had visited all the secret test sites agreed that DA trips to Dugway were the neediest of all need-to-know travel. It was the opaquest of any military installation, they said. Compared to Dugway, Nevada's Area 51 and the Mercury Test Site were the next best things to all-inclusive tropical resorts. This was for good reason, too; they said that on cold winter nights when the wind was calm and the moon was full, the plaintive bleats of the ghosts of the 6,000 sheep[24] could still be heard at Dugway.

"You're going up on Friday." Bernie continued, "You'll fly up to Salt Lake on Friday, rent a car, run out to Dugway with a packet, make sure it goes to the right guy, do what he tells you to do, and then fly home. "

Jerome thought this was strange because travel time on Friday would eat the whole day and Saturday work was unusual in the realm of Bernie. Bernie read Jerome's doubts, though, so Bernie preempted all of Jerome's ambivalence by uttering the magic words, "It's all Top Secret." Bernie said he'd have Della cut the travel arrangements by Thursday noon.

---

[24] On March 13, 1968, approximately 6,000 sheep were found dead in Skull Valley, 27 miles east of a VX gas test site on the Dugway Proving Grounds. The wind had been out of the west. The US Army first categorically denied any toxic substance from the Proving Grounds was involved, but soon after (in 1997) admitted to some possibility of guilt.

Then, as a postscript, Bernie added that his daughter was a second-year student at Brigham Young. The meals in her dorm were boring, so would Jerome do another favor and take his daughter to dinner at a restaurant? Written, Bernie's words read like a favor request. Spoken, Bernie's words were heard like an order.

Since Provo wasn't right on the road from the Salt Lake Airport to Dugway, Bernie told Jerome, "Just run south to Provo, take Kathy to dinner, and then catch route 73 west out of American Fork, follow that over to 199, and 199 runs right into Dugway. It isn't over ten miles farther than straight west on I-80. Won't cost the company more than an extra gallon of gas. And put the dinner on the company tab. Oh, and don't say anything about this to anyone but Della. "

Bernie pulled a framed picture out of the filing cabinet. "This is my wife and Kathy," he said, waving his hand at the photo. "I have a son, too, but he's off doing mission work." The picture showed Bernie standing between two women, both almost as tall as he. On his right was a dour brunette in a long dark skirt and a pale blue sweater. On his left stood a lovely, vivacious blonde in an emerald green sheath. She was the stereotypical BYU coed; she was bright, smiling, and oh so fresh and pretty. "Kathy will be looking forward to having a nice dinner for a change. Any questions?"

"What a beautiful family!" Jerome exclaimed. He left Bernie's office excited beyond words. Top Secret! A huge step up the ladder of success! Being trusted to take the boss' beautiful daughter to dinner, and sanctioned to write it off besides! Woowoo! I am IN the inner circle!

Remark: Jerome thought he was doing Bernie a favor, and he was, but it was by allowing himself to be hooked so easily. Bernie just needs reel him in.

Jerome's excitement first gave way to anxiety about driving a rental car over mountain back roads from Provo to Dugway and then turned to agony and angst about what he'd have to do at Dugway and secure handling the Top-Secret packet. His mind was still running amok and his Thursday morning coffee still too hot to drink when his phone rang. It was Kathy. "Jerome. This is Kathy. Daddy said you are coming up to Utah tomorrow."

Jerome brightened right up. "Yes, I am. He asked me to stop by Provo to take you to dinner tomorrow evening. I'm looking forward to meeting you."

"And you're taking me to dinner Saturday evening, too. Daddy said you could stay Friday night in Provo, run over to Dugway Saturday morning and do whatever it is, and be back to Provo by dinner time Saturday. Just look at your travel arrangements. Daddy said it's all set up."

What a pleasant surprise! This was a good deal getting better! Kathy assured him that all was in order, gave him her phone number, and directions to her dorm. He just had to give her a call while getting his rental car in Salt Lake. She repeated the request. "Jerome, you **must** call me from the airport."

Jerome picked up the sealed plain brown wrapper packet from Della. Security was easy; just keep it in the briefcase, lock the briefcase in the car trunk if not in his hand, and avoid breaking the seal. His travel plan was just as Kathy said.

Jerome called Kathy the minute he got the car. She told him the route to take and about signing her out at the dorm. She gushed about getting away from dorm food and how Daddy was SO happy that Jerome could find time in his busy schedule to take Daddy's little girl to dinner.

But then she had a teeny tiny request. "I just love Irish Cream liqueur over French vanilla ice cream, but there aren't any liquor stores in Provo and I have no way to get to Salt Lake to buy it—would you be a darling and get me a little bitty bottle of Irish Cream? One of the tiny ones? Oh, please, please! I'd love you forever. Daddy will never ever know." The liquor store in Salt Lake happened to be right on his route to Provo.

Jerome dutifully picked up a wee mickey of Irish Cream, drove down to Provo, and checked into the motel. At 6:30 he drove to Kathy's dorm. A tall grumpy brunette woman was waiting beside the sign-out desk. She wore a pale blue sweater and a long dark skirt. Jerome was about to ask her to call Kathy's room when he recognized the blue sweater. Then he recalled the frowning face in the family photo. Oopski! Mormon women just don't show their age.

Kathy had the tiny bottle into her purse before the car door closed. In the restaurant, she ate well. Jerome came to understand why Kathy's was an ample figure. After dinner, she requested a tenth-sized flask of vodka. Jerome was to pick up the jar on the way back from Dugway.

The run to Dugway was hot and dusty and the road from the town of Dugway to the entrance of the Proving Grounds as spooky and stark as a desert scene in *The Twilight Zone*. The packet was addressed to Mr. James Brown at the C14 guard station. The guard at C14 looked at Jerome suspiciously, and grunted "more crap for Brown" into the phone.

A suit and tie type appeared to claim the packet. He handed Jerome a receipt, assured Jerome that Mr. Brown would indeed get the packet, and ordered Jerome to get back into the car, make a U turn, and promptly leave the installation or face immediate imprisonment in a federal facility for Section 8B felony trespassing. Jerome fled via the way he'd come not fifteen minutes earlier.

Jerome picked up the vodka and drove back to Provo, tired and disconcerted. Why so much expense for doing so little? The only explanation was that the packet had to be of the very highest importance. The receipt signature was illegible and the name on the suit's badge was taped over, but surely the suit must have been Mr. Brown himself.

As Kathy slipped the jar of hooch into her massive purse, she thanked Jerome with a kiss on the cheek. She had Beef Wellington. It took until a quarter to forever for her to eat it. On the way back to the dorm she said she'd be late for curfew, but this was her best date ever.

At the dorm desk Jerome started to say they were late because he'd been to Dugway, but the dorm mother hushed him. Being a few minutes late because of national security was not a problem. Kathy was right again. "Dugway" was a magic word. Dugway excuses were not to be questioned.

Bernie thanked Jerome on Monday, commenting that Kathy thought he was a very nice, proper, and handsome young man. And, as Bernie said to do, Jerome filled out his expense voucher, including the receipts for the dinners with Kathy. Per her suggestion, the costs of the booze became parking fees. Jerome's signature asserted that all of the expenses were legitimate business expenditures. Della did her part, too, by duly filing a full set of copies of Jerome's expense reports.

Lesson 5.1: Jerome doesn't know it yet, but he has become Bernie's boy. He's been reeled in, and by signing the expense voucher, he has gaffed himself.

Six weeks later Jerome was sent to Utah on another charade. He had to bring along a tenth of 190 proof grain spirits. Kathy was delighted.

A month later, Bernie send Jerome forth again. Kathy called for a fifth of vodka. She met Jerome wearing a super chaste button-to-the-throat blouse and a very long skirt. On their way out of the dorm, she introduced Jerome as "a dear friend" to three coed friends right after she gave him a not-at-all-sisterly kiss.

Kathy chose the restaurant and the chardonnay. When the waiter asked if she was 21, she said she had forgotten her ID and suggested that Jerome order just a glass of the chardonnay. Jerome didn't get more than a taste of his wine, though. And none from his second or third glass. The dinner was fine, large, and expensive.   Kathy found need to lean against Jerome on the way to the car but somehow steadied herself well enough to put down a straight belt of the vodka while Jerome was walking around to the driver's side of the car.

Preoccupied with how he was going to get the obviously drunk girl past the front desk radar, Jerome was unprepared for parking lot drama. The moment he turned off the ignition, Kathy was sprawled across him, her head on his lap, and her arms around his neck. She had most of the buttons on her blouse undone and her skirt was somehow laid open to her waist. Everything was ghostly white – her chest was white, her bra was white, her bare belly was white, her legs were white, and her panties were white. Kathy was wearing her Big Girl panties. But she always wore them. She had to, because she was a big girl.

Kathy yanked Jerome's head down as if to make him kiss her, but his forehead bounced off the horn ring. The horn blared.

A heartbeat later a flashlight was beaming into the car and a cop was bellowing, **"What's going on in here?"**

Kathy crawled off Jerome and sat up. She made a show out of refastening the three decorative safety pins that were supposed to hold the slit on her long skirt closed, buttoning her blouse, and straightening herself out.

The cop made a show of recording the license plate, getting a look at Jerome's driver's license, and loudly thanking God that he'd arrived in time to rescue the fair maiden's virtue.

Clutching her big purse to her chest so the vodka bottle wouldn't rattle, Kathy shooed the cop away and headed for the dorm. The cop told Jerome that if he ever caught Jerome making a right turn without signaling on the campus, he'd personally ensure that Jerome would be charged with criminal trespass and the felony sexual assault charges reinstated.

Lesson 5.2: Jerome has become Kathy's and Bernie's boy. Kathy has Jerome hooked, reeled in, and gaffed.

On Jerome's flight back to Albuquerque his worries turned his mouth to dry flannel and his skivvies to wet flannel. What happened in the dorm? Had she been caught drunk? Surely, they could have smelled the alcohol. What if they found the bottle in her purse? And what was this about not having an ID? Was she not yet 21? She'd told him she was almost 22, but in retrospect, nearly 22 was old for the second year of college. Thinking that Mormon youths had to serve as missionaries, he'd not given it a second thought when she'd mentioned her age. But maybe only the young men were missionaries?

Lesson 5.3: Naiveté is such a marvelous force.

Kathy called Monday. When Jerome asked if she got into the dorm okay, her response was scornful. "What? Do you think I'm a goody two shoes moron like you? I had my roommate open a first-floor window. So now I owe her. When you come to Provo on Friday, you are bringing a fifth of vodka for me and a fifth of 151-proof dark Bacardi for my roommate." At that, Jerome broke off the call, saying that he was late for a meeting and that he'd have to call her back.

Until this time, poor Jerome hoped that Kathy was just a little drunk and horny, but now he realized that Kathy's thirst was his problem. If the booze wasn't already linked to him, it would be, and the cop had his name from the parking lot. What if he got nailed for providing alcohol to a minor? Felony sexual assault?

When Bernie came by to tell Jerome to go to Salt Lake on Friday, Jerome lied, saying that he had a dental appointment. Bernie got unhappy.

Kathy was on the phone in minutes. "You **will** come to Provo," she said, "**with** the bottle of vodka for me and the rum for my roommate, or I'm telling Daddy that you tried to take advantage of my innocence. Don't forget that the cop in the parking lot saw plenty." Jerome lied again, saying okay, he'd be in Provo on schedule.

It was time to break his pledge of silence. Jerome explained things to John in complete detail. They agreed that with the possible illegal provision of alcohol to a minor, Jerome's name on the dorm sign-out sheets, the presumed guilt in the faux sex scene in the dorm parking lot, and Bernie's temper, Jerome's only viable option was to get the hell out of Dodge. He'd mail in his resignation.

So he did. And John lost a highly skilled, technically able, and honorable guy who was now less gullible for the Kathy experience.

Bernie dropped by John's office the next morning. Word was already out that Jerome was gone. "I hear Jerome is now a former employee," Bernie commented in a conversational tone.

"Yes, he resigned. I received his resignation letter this morning, so I sent his original letter to Personnel and made a copy for you. It's in the company mail," John responded.

"It's too bad he's gone, but he didn't meet with me to resign. So," Bernie chuckled, "he left no forwarding address. I can't send him his July paycheck, his reimbursement for travel, or refund his retirement deposits. I guess we can forget about his unused vacation, too. Really too bad." After pausing to gloat for a moment, Bernie asked, "Do you have a young single guy who can do some traveling this weekend? I need a trustworthy guy to take some highly classified stuff to Dugway."

John had no nominees. That afternoon John learned that Bernie had found a guy in Marketing who was itching to travel to Salt Lake.

Jerome had fled to El Paso. The next Monday he scored a job interview with a small company that was into engineering tech services for the White Sands Missile Range. That evening he called John. He gave John his new El Paso address and said that he was the most recently employed engineer in El Paso. He closed by asking John to wish him luck, because he'd been promised a chance at a manager's slot in a year.

John sent Jerome's forwarding address to Payroll, so the termination checks were duly forwarded to Jerome. If Bernie ever learned that John provided the forwarding address, he never commented on it to John.

Lesson 5.4: Remember this when the shit hits the fan — your boss can always afford the better raincoat.

Remark: Doing what the boss wants done is a good idea unless the boss requires you to cut corners. If he forces you to cut corners, make sure you don't cut the corners off your ass shield.

So, what are your options when the boss wants you to stretch the rules? One is raising an objection as soon as the boss suggests it. This is good, because it shows you are listening to what the boss is saying, and that you aren't eager to be compromised. At least not until the pot is sweetened, anyway.

But things like rule changes can sneak up on you. Keeping a log with lots of quotations and dates with clock times might help. And remember, it's usually possible to reconstruct *what* happened but *why* it happened is usually unknown, so the log should emphasize the whys. If they are so labeled, even conjectures on whys are helpful.

On the other side of the ledger, the boss had damn well better listen when an underling objects to taking a shortcut. The boss should expect that a log, replete with quotations, memos, phone calls, and gory details will be kept. And, that one day, the log will be shared.

Chapter 6

Choosing New Managers

From your perspective, does it appear that senior management cares not one rip about management below their lofty levels on the company ladder? If so, you may be surprised to learn that senior managers actually care a lot about how you fill entry-level management positions. It's just that they're so wretchedly clever about waiting to state their non-negotiable demands until an instant before you extend an offer to your chosen person. In stark contrast, mid-level managers eagerly provide vast quantities of often conflicting advice as you strive to fill your entry-level opening.

So, you have too much near-above directive and your far-above guidance is tardy, sparse, and filtered by your near-above management. Nobody except you seems to be interested in filling the spot with someone who will actually get your job done. So, which voice of authority calls the shots? Your boss' boss, your boss, you, or the demands of the job?

To run unscathed through this gauntlet, you will need to make careful preparations, take clever or even cunning actions, and hone your selective hearing skills.

The task of concern

The junior-to-low-mid-level manager is likely to be a player in efforts to fill entry-level management positions. Such a scenario might be like this: Your boss has charged you with finding and hiring a manager to fill a leadership position in your burgeoning section. This new manager will take over some of the tasks you are now doing in lieu of having free evenings, weekends, holidays and vacations. Your secret hope is that you'll find someone who will eventually completely replace you and you'll move up the ladder, or, if out the door, to a way better job.

Let's see about this issue. The following exhibit sketches a process for filling an entry-level management job.

Exhibit 2

Management Selection Flowchart

1. Establish all necessary credentials		Go to 2
2. Compile wish list; draft job description (JD)		Go to 3
3. Reduce wish list to needed skills		Go to 4
4. Revisit and update job JD		Go to 5
5. Post job, do internal candidate search		Go to 6
6. Prune internal candidate list		Go to 7
7. Recycle 1-6 until internals are bona fide		Go to 8
8. Prefer outsider to internals?	Yes	Go to 9
	No	Go to 10
9. Accept recruiter's nominees?	Yes	Go to 11
	No[25]	Go to 8
10. More than one in-house bona fide?	Yes	Go to 11
	No	Go to 13
11. Choose selection procedure		
Interviews?		Go to 12
HR procedure?		Go to 12
12. Revisit all of above until consensus		Go to 13
13. Select the new manager, put the newbie to work		

In theory, you could just follow through the steps in this exhibit and get the job done. In real life there always are a few rough joints between steps.

---

[25] After a couple cycles of preferring outsider but rejecting recruiter nominees, the Step 8 Yes will turn into a No.

Case Study — A management selection by HR procedure

The case study shown here came about as a result of Bernie remoting[26] Maurice. While this example is rich with illustrations, the perils of promotions bogged things down and turned the project into a tangled mess. So, as a road map to help you wade through the confusion, the numbered items from the Exhibit are utilized as headlines below.

1. Establish all necessary credentials

The new manager was to take over management of about half of John's section; a half-dozen systems people, a couple junior programmers, a gofer, and an apprentice gofer. Although Mo was being replaced and he had reported through Cy, Bernie claimed the opening. It seemed Cy was getting too big for his britches. Then, to put the screws to John, too, Bernie declared that this new manager would be **a man** who reported to John but of course had a dotted line to Bernie. There was no assigned admin, so like John, the newbie would have to borrow, beg, steal, or use his body to get admin help from the typing pool.

Bernie viewed the hiring as a simple, low-cost refill of a very small pair of shoes. "You don't know what you are doing, so I'm going to guide you and make it easy for you, Johnny Boy," Bernie advised. "With Cyrus around, you don't need a guy with experience. All the new guy needs to know is when to ask questions and when to keep his mouth shut." And then Bernie added for the benefit of all within earshot,

---

[26] Promote = kick up the ladder, Demote = kick down the ladder, Remote = kick clear off the ladder.

"Mo didn't do diddly, so even a woman would be an improvement." Della recorded that statement in her "Bernie said" file.

Lesson 6.1: Once entrenched in a hierarchy, a dud manager can stink up the place almost forever if the higher-ups don't expect him to smell good.

Remark: By announcing that he had minimal expectations for the new manager, Bernie did John no favor.

2. Compile wish list of skills, draft job description (JD)

John assembled all the calls for wants and needs for the new manager's services. Notably, John received no input from management above Bernie's rung on the ladder. John blithely assumed that Bernie had not filtered out input from higher levels. John also assumed a mere update of Mo's old JD was needed.

3. Reduce wish list to needed skills, revise JD

With the new JD in place, job specs written, and expecting approvals at any moment, John prepared the job posting. The job posting was set to appear on Monday morning. Just before quitting time on Friday disaster struck. A message left on John's phone said that the CEO required a dragon slayer. Someone from The Above had called Bernie, telling him to order John to hire Bob, the CEO's "Heavy Hitter". In a state of panic, John dashed into Bernie's office to confer, but it being Friday afternoon, Bernie was already gone to the Polish Ballet.

Per usual, with Bernie gone, Della had scurried out the door. But in her haste, she hadn't locked Bob's curriculum vitae (CV) into Bernie's CLASSIFIED safe. The CV was lying face up on her desk. So, John copied it. When he compared Bob's surprisingly sketchy CV and credentials with the job specs and job description, Bob was stunningly lacking. This spurred John into serious detective work. Upon investigation, it turned out that the "Heavy Hitter" was the CEO's admin's dog walker.

Lesson 6.2: If John had not had the job description into HR for approval, he'd been forced to hire the trophy guy. You can't count on luck, but you can fight unrealistic management demands with technology.

Remark: It's good luck to have a bullet-proof job description on file, but you may need to make your own luck. If the boss wants you to hire a latter-day Saint George, counter by having your best candidates load the latest release of "Death to Dragons" on their smart phones. Then tell the boss that any of your choices will cost less than his trophy and in fact will be better, because they have cutting edge dragon-killing technology.

4. Revisit job description

John 's do-over of Mo's JD was enough to stymie Bob, but the JD was so out of date and hopelessly dumbed down that even the HR rep understood the tech stuff! Another revision of the JD was in order. Checking to ensure the JD was in strict adherence to the HR guidelines was needed, too.

The JD thing had a happy ending; after sorting out the wishes and then compiling and condensing the needs, John was pleased to find that his new JD did in fact span the spectrum of tasks that he could reasonably ask the new manager to perform.

5. Post job, do internal candidate search

After the Bob fiasco, John got the job opening duly posted, but the only guy in the company who actually applied for the job was Elwood. Woody was a hard worker and okay technically, but he was utterly oblivious of the work and workers around him. You know the type—the guy with so little leadership talent that he'd have trouble convincing Titanic passengers to follow him into a life boat.

6. Prune candidate list

John did not have to prune because there were no bona fide and qualified applicants.

7. Recycle above steps until candidates are bona fide

There was no hope for poor Woody, so it was all kicked back to Bernie's desk.

8. Prefer outsider?

For sure, Bernie wanted an outsider. He announced some constraints, though:

"I'm tossing the applications from experienced outside applicants. Experienced outsiders applying for an entry-level management job are just a bunch of clowns who've crapped in their nests and now want a clean sand box."

"I don't want an inexperienced outsider, either. Our business is product development, not manager development."

Bernie's unstated constraint was that the premium cost of an outside hire was charged to Bernie's discretionary spending pot, and Bernie's annual bonus was the discretionary pot residue.

9. Accept recruiter's nominees?

Bernie's go-to guy, Paul the Procurer, sent a list of nominees anyway. And Bernie rejected the entire list. It might have been that Paul had tried to dump a loser on Bernie during their last go-around. Or, it might have been that the unsubstantiated rumor was true; Bernie was unhappy with Paul because Paul had shorted Bernie on a kickback.

In any case, it was back to Step 8 and reconsidering insiders.

10. More than one in-house candidate?

Claiming he wanted their help, Bernie called Cy, Lawrence, and John to a decision meeting. What should they do since there were no viable in-house candidates?

Bernie opened the meeting by denying that he had anyone tabbed for the job. He steepled his fingertips and sat back. "I once had a leader who groomed an heir-apparent," Bernie recalled. "The chosen one was guided up the golden staircase into ever-higher realms of responsibility. With uncertainty banished, everyone knew exactly how to suck up." Bernie took a long pause and then added, "It took the loss of me and half the staff" — long sigh — "before my former boss finally figured out that I didn't agree with his choice of heir."

Lesson 6.3: If your goal is to rid your department of every high performing young lion except the fair-haired one, grooming an heir works even better than managerial selection via the eeny-meeny-miney-mo or rock-paper-scissors methods.

Bernie secretly favored Cy's competent but annoying and super-cynical guy, Adolph. However, Adolph was so despised that Bernie knew he'd have a firestorm on his hands if the blame for promoting Adolph was laid at his doorstep.

"So," Bernie beamed[27], "I've got a great idea. Internal applicants are not a problem. I'll give you three guys to choose from." Bernie held out his right palm toward John to silence him and said to Cy and Lawrence, "I'll name a guy who will apply. You two will each name a guy who will apply. Just tell them that Bernie says they either step up to the plate or Woody gets the job by default. Woody will be even worse than Mo."

---

[27] It is good to note the context when the diabolical boss smiles in that special way.

Suddenly, there were three in-house candidates; Adolph(A) and Beedolph[28](B), from Cy's staff, and Lawrence's guy Ceedolph(C).

11. Choice of selection procedure?

Interviews?

Bernie's usual interview procedure was to enlist a bevy of senior staff members as an interview panel. Since Bernie took great pleasure from browbeating interviewees, he interviewed the candidates as well. Then, after the panel's interviews were completed, he'd call a meeting of the panel members and have even more fun browbeating the panel guys. Not surprisingly, Bernie's favored candidate was selected for the job almost every time.

The HR procedure?

But Bernie's interview process took a couple weeks to complete and he wanted to go see the shows in Las Vegas. Realizing that he'd be totally in the clear if perception held HR responsible for promoting Adolph, Bernie offered the project to HR as a trial run of their new management skills assessment workshop.

Bernie figured he couldn't miss; the HR procedure would very likely name Adolph the winner, and if not, Bernie could quietly subvert "the erroneous HR decision" to ensure HR's sanction of Adolph.

---

[28] To avoid appearing to play favorites, Bernie "randomly" labeled his guy as A, leaving B and C for the other candidates. Still smarting from losing control, Cy dubbed the other candidates "Beedolph" and "Ceedolph"

Late on Friday afternoon, Bernie informed John that he was to participate in a management assessment workshop commencing at 8:00 AM on Monday morning. John was to report to HR at 7:00 AM for a preparation briefing.

John supposed that his co-assessors Lawrence and Cy knew what management assessment workshops were. He hoped so, because he sure as hell didn't.

The HR process had been developed by and was managed by D, the CHWDRHD. The procedure created a systematically defined skills assessment score.

According to R, who was the Workshop Note Keeper and Recorder (WNKR) and D's assistant, this process would home right in on personality traits that correlated closely with excellent management and leadership skills. Indeed, in the preliminary testing, the process had in fact proven to be quite effective at identifying individuals who got high scores in systematically defined skills assessments.

But there was even more good news! HR was enthralled with the defined skills process because their system reduced the mounds of psychobabble data to machine-readable form. Further, the WNKR's customized analytical software created data structures that facilitated comparisons and produced a plethora of evaluation scores.

These scores swept away all vestiges of reliance on gut instinct, the dreaded archenemy of objectivity. Some would add that reliance on reason was reduced to an even greater extent.

The first day of the workshop was uneventful; although the tasks were simple, the get-acquainted exercises generated many forms and massive amounts of data.

The workshop's flagship exercise began early Tuesday morning. Candidates A, B and C were supposed to role play as D's manager. The candidates were given the rules and written instructions but told to wing it script-wise. D was to follow a fixed script. The candidates were to meet 1-on-1 with D to identify the critical issues underlying D's several alleged performance shortfalls. In the afternoon, A, B and C were to separately collaborate with D to chart a course to remedy D's failings.

In Wednesday morning, A's, B's and C's draft comprehensive plans to correct D's performance were to be discussed with D. The plans were to be agreed upon and finalized in candidate, assessors, CHWDRHD, and WNKR meetings scheduled on Wednesday afternoon and Thursday.

R handed A, B and C the packets of material for their preparations for the simulated course correction meetings. After D stated that the first guy to go into the barrel had two hours to prepare for his 1-on-1 meeting, R and D excused themselves and retired to their well-appointed offices.

A closed his packet and set it aside after just a few minutes. He had another cup of coffee, a sweet roll, and took a little nap instead of doing more prepping. It was clear that A dismissed the exercise as a trivial farce, so it was not surprising that A declared that he'd be the first to go into the 1-on-1 meeting with D.

D appeared at the conference room promptly at 10:00 AM. A joined him, D hung the "Do Not Disturb" sign on the doorknob, and firmly closed the door.

With B and C still busily preparing, the workshop suite grew quiet except for the rising sounds of vigorous conversation coming from the conference room. Cy and

Lawrence soon left, having better things to do than make coffee for WNKR and CHWDRHD. John was less rank than Cy or Lawrence, so he was assigned to operate the coffee pot.

John got drowsy, having been up until 2:00 AM working on the myriad first day assessments. He drained the last cup of coffee from the urn but the coffee was stale. It was almost as bitter as alimony payments, so he set a fresh pot to brewing. Having drunk almost no coffee, when he sat down, he dozed off.

Shortly after 10:30 AM, D screamed, "You can't do that!" so loudly that it roused John. A emerged from the conference room a moment later, wearing what we crude country folk would call a shit-eating grin. He dusted off his hands and chuckled. Then, winking at John, he said, "I fired the son of a bitch."

As A headed toward the snack room for a cup of coffee and the last sweet roll, D burst out of the conference room. His face was lavender and his voice a high-pitched squeal. He yelled at John, saying that the 1-on-1 sessions with B and C were postponed. Then, acidly observing the Cy-Lawrence absence, D said he was taking the rest of the day off, too. "R's in charge," D growled, well to the high side of huffy as he went out the door.

In the dark of Wednesday morning, D was ambulanced to the ER with a cerebral hemorrhage[29]. It was brought on, the doctors thought, by stress-related hypertension. D didn't live long enough to start rehab.

---

[29] Once upon a time, this cerebrovascular accident would have been called a "fit of apoplexy".

12. Revisit all above until consensus reached

The last three days of the management assessment workshop were cancelled. A formally withdrew from candidacy. It was unclear whether his withdrawal was on his own volition or if it was prompted by the advice of others. In the wreckage of the workshop, Bernie grudgingly consented to a probationary promotion for B. B would get no second chances if he screwed up, Bernie declared.

13. Congratulate, put the new manager to work

Follow-up or fall-out, take your pick

After D's funeral, Bernie called a meeting "to get to the bottom of this", i.e., affix blame. Bernie, Cy, Lawrence, John, Della, A, and R (just promoted from WNKR to Deputy Management Workshop Trainer (DMWT) and now acting CHWDRHD), were invited to the meeting. B and C were excluded for reasons that Bernie did not share.

Bernie opened the meeting with a question. "Why do you people still blame A when it was all D's fault because he took his exercise too seriously?" Bernie had hoped for agreement by acclamation but wasn't surprised when R objected vehemently.

But Bernie had his ducks in a line — he'd secretly studied up on the *Chemin de Fer* Consensus Builder[30]. In a row across the top of the chalkboard, Bernie wrote the names

---

[30] The French words "Chemin de Fer" translate literally as "Way of Iron" but idiomatically the expression means "Railroad". It's also the name of a Las Vegas high stakes card game very similar to baccarat.

Bernie, Della, Cy, Lawrence, A, D, and John. He then put a column of seven chalk marks under each name.

Bernie took the lead, declaring that he, Della and A were not responsible. He erased one chalk mark under each of the names Bernie, Della and A. Bernie asked Della to vote. She agreed with Bernie; she, Bernie and A were blameless. So, Bernie erased another chalk mark for Bernie, A and Della. Cy and Lawrence spoke as one, saying neither of them were to blame, so two chalk marks for Cy and Lawrence vanished.

When Bernie called on A to vote, R jumped up and shouted, "D was not to blame! It was all A's fault!" A rose and left the room in a huff. Bernie erased one mark under D.

All the while this had been going on, Bernie had been glancing at the clock and debating every word and point. So, when it finally came time for John to speak, there were only a few minutes left in the hour and Bernie shushed him.

Bernie totaled the votes. It was clear that he, Della, Cy, Lawrence and A were the least culpable, because they each had only 5 marks left. D had only partial guilt, because he had 6 marks left, and John was obviously the guiltiest because he still had all 7 of his marks. R was pleased to have D mostly exonerated, and vowed to duly record John's role in the tragedy on John's permanent HR file.

John objected on the grounds that he'd not had an opportunity to vote, but Bernie said that could hardly be a valid concern because A was absent so he didn't get a vote either.

Lesson 6.4: Being the last speaker is the best spot on the agenda, but only if you actually get to speak.

Remark: Oh, one more thing. The audience has to actually listen, too. To you.

Remark: Bernie came into the meeting with an excellent plan.
- He wrote John on the board last so he'd vote last, and then dawdled to keep John from voting.
- Had A not stormed out of the meeting, R would not have been allowed to vote, either.
- Bernie brought Della along, knowing she would vote with him on every point.
- Bernie did not invite B or C because he could not control their votes.
- Bernie's final master's touch was to set the questioning template by asking who specifically was innocent rather than who was guilty. As a rule, people first cover their own ass and then accuse others.

Remark: D had thrown his heart and soul and mortgaged his career prospects on his assessment system. He was assiduously playing by the rules and had never considered that participants would not play his game by the rules (that is, his rules plus the company rules). In the real world, some people are reluctant to play by their own rules, let alone someone else's arbitrarily imposed, constricting rules. A knew company policies about firings but the pleasure of pushing D's buttons was a greater reward for him than being promoted.

Lesson 6.5: You can't count on people playing by your rules.

Remark: Transforming a notion into a numerical score can make the notion seem to turn into a fact, and it's way easier to get your way by using numbers instead of ideas. Bernie's *Chemin de Fer* Consensus Maker transmogrified gut level preferences and opinions into numbers. Similarly, the management assessment process produced numerical scores from thoughts and feelings.

Lesson 6.6: **If you can transform a vague notion into a numerical score, you greatly improve your chances of convincing skeptics that the vague notion is factual.**

Remark: Evaluators and processes are powerful tools. Powerful tools can be manipulated to achieve powerful ends. No doubt D knew how to subtly tweak his management assessment exercises to shade the promotion process. The ability to sway promotions is potentially lucrative—some said that D dreamed of the day when most of the managers in the company would be beholden to his selection process. If so, D wanted to own the shoulder that governed the arm that controlled the hand that rocked the cradle.

Lesson 6.7: **Summarizing scores must always be examined with healthy skepticism.**

Lesson 6.8: **Think carefully about needs when you decide about promotions.**

Remark: If you need only a nose tackle, do you have the resolve to resist drafting a possible future Hall of Fame wide receiver who will score tons of touchdowns? When for way less money you could have that ugly, 365-pounder who waddles instead of runs, is utterly immovable except when he chooses to move, is quicker from down to up than a whore's drawers, and is the meanest guy around?

Chapter 7

Managing Your Manager

Movies and television depict managing the manager as the exclusive domain of sexy secretaries with trophy-class mammaries. The managers are depicted as easily manipulated lecherous old men. No doubt it does happen this way, but we insist there are other ways to manage a manager from below. We're not claiming it's easy, but common folks are managing their managers every day. It's time to take a hard look at what's involved:

First, what could lead you to managing your manager? There are two likely case scenarios:

Case 1) Providing or enabling his indulgences in private forbidden pleasures. The manager's killer T cells provide him no immunity to wine, women, or song, so he needs your camouflage 60/24/7/52/10+[31] to maintain (or enhance) his vice. Discrete, comprehensive, and very timely services are required. Lollygagging over tea and crumpets in Nepal is not allowed when your boss spends the night in dissipated bliss and awakens to the need of a cover story at 7 AM. It's worse still if he's a way-past-his-prime stud muffin; you may have just minutes to fabricate a cover-up for the man so desperate for that one last fling that he throws caution aside.

---

[31] 60 minutes/hour, 24 hours/day, 7 days/week, 52 weeks/year, for 10+ years.

Case 2) Doing his work while enabling him to take the credit for the work. Eventually, he'll become unable to fully perform his job without your help and you may become indispensable by performing tasks that are his non-delegable obligations. You thus may be able, and possibly may even be forced, to manage your manager.

In either case, the reward for your service is a certain level of control over the manager's thoughts and deeds.

Comparing Case 1 with Case 2, failings of the flesh are way more newsworthy, much less common, and far, far more fun than shortfalls in managerial performance.

We instinctively understand failings of the flesh, but the roots of waning managerial performance require examination: The most commonly encountered situations here are leaders with lamentable cognitive deficits. The shortfalls may be in learning new processes or keeping track of details. A major class of failings arise from gaffers who resist innovations and their geezer anologs who insist nothing gets fixed if it isn't broken. And beyond your basic gaffing and geezing, there are those who are making daily forays into the frontiers of dotage. These old farts have ongoing management tasks that they once did well but are now beyond them. Or beneath them. Or maybe leave them beside themselves. Whatever.

In all these situations, the failing manager may have no choice except to appeal for continuing aid from a discrete white knight. White knights are in high demand today and the demographics of today's workplace suggest this demand will only grow.

Although the services you would perform in the situations described above are dramatically different, in all cases your burden of service is heavy and unending. And, because you must bear these heavy and unending burdens, heavy and unending costs are incurred.

An economic model for managing the manager

We have come to the word "costs". Let us cut the crap and put our cards on the table with the faces up. Managing your manager is business. However altruistic you and your manager may be, if you manage your manager, you will be driven into a quid pro quo situation.

Some will think that speaking of costs vis-a-vis managing their manager is indelicate, like hiring an escort. We don't see it that way at all; it's not like hiring an escort, it's like being an escort.

Setting sensitivities aside, we'll handle this in a professional manner. Treating it as a business arrangement actually turns out to be quite helpful, because it allows us to apply the *quid pro quo* economic model. "Quid pro quo" translates literally as "this for that". One thing in exchange for another. So, to manage your manager, you need:

- A quid. You alone can offer your boss a service at a cost your boss deems acceptable.

- A pro. The pro is your lever to motivate the exchange. Your boss must be induced to exchange what he has for what you can provide. To be useful, levers must have a fulcrum.

- A quo. This is a benefit you want.

Quos are your choice. They are varied as the fish in the sea, but certain rules apply:

- First, your boss must have the capacity to dispense the quo you covet. If he lacks this resource, there is no point in attempting to manage your manager.

- Second, your boss must have autonomy. Micromanagement from above is incompatible with management from below. It just won't do to have your boss second-guessed on your self-serving decision.

- Third, your quo must not generate dissension among your peers. Word always gets out among the peers when one of their own gets a special bennie. This pretty much takes out dollar perks like big bonuses and raises, but the door is wide open for bennies with under-the-radar price tags.

Do not begin your manage-the-manager crusade until you have a quid to demonstrate to your boss, there is leverage at hand to make your boss want to accept your quid, and you hold a clearly defined quo in mind.

Case Study 1 — A successful management of a manager

Bernie's office staff situation widens the envelope on the classic situation of an administrative assistant successfully managing the manager.

Bernie brought old Della along as part of the allowed package of perks when he hired in at Desert Aromatics. This led John to be pretty sure that she'd held Bernie by the short hairs for a long, long time.

But when the Bernie/Della arrangement began is immaterial. What's important is that Della understood Bernie's long-standing insatiable needs to gaze upon naked women. Without explicitly approving or condoning his vice, she enabled him through an elaborate system of excuse provision, two-calendar time accounting, and creation of synthetic tasks. In return for her exceptional service, Della was granted the departmental chair of queen bee in perpetuity.

Lesson 7.1: Glaring, wrinkled, grumpy old Della is proof that you don't have to be sexy, young, and pretty to boss your boss.

Remark: In fact, being a Fair Elaine is probably a handicap, because every word and action of pretty young ladies will be scrutinized by older, less comely, or by the even more critical eyes of no-longer-favored women.

Della's quid is as stated, and her pro is clear. It's worth noting that Della's quo was not likely to attract attention from the HR rules pixies or from accounting. The accountants were too busy with forestalling salary increases and disputing nickel/dime expense account chits, anyway. Della went unchallenged among the other admins, too, because she was older, more wrinkled, a relentless stickler for details, and she certainly had a queen bee persona. She wanted only status, and you can't put a price tag on status.

Case Study 2: Management of the manager that failed in spite of everything

Sid was a contract oversight officer with responsibility for placement and performance evaluations for several multi-million-dollar projects. Sid was in fact a doddering old fool, but he had the correct initials after his name and he smelled of woolens, questionable hygiene, and a sour Meerschaum pipe. Plus, he talked a good game at cocktail parties. So, to the casual acquaintance, he looked, smelled, and sounded like a foremost authority on virtually any topic. He was beloved among the contractors because he was a world class glad-hander who was sure to send the contract their way if they flattered him. Away from cocktail parties and meetings with the contractors, Sid spent his every hour of each workday channeling the south end of a Shetland pony[32] stallion.

Glen reported to Sid. Glen took care of background checking on the contractors, did all the contract follow-up work, reviewed all the output from the contractors, and did the dirty work of managing corrective actions. In short, Glen took all the unpleasant work and virtually all of the real work off Sid's desk, while Sid blithely claimed credit for it all. It is fair to say that Sid could not have performed his job for a single afternoon without Glen's help. But Glen was essentially locked into Sid's assistant's chair by two kids in college and a big mortgage.

---

[32] Shetland ponies are not really ponies. They are miniature draft horses—cute, fuzzy, amazingly strong for their size, and possibly more obstinate than mules.

Given that Glen was performing as the de facto manager and had been for several years, could he improve his situation by managing his manager? Glen had the quid (his excellent and all-encompassing support for Sid's projects), a pro (Glen's understanding of Sid's deplorable incompetence) and a quo (Glen's simple wish of being recognized and fairly compensated as an outstanding contract oversight assistant). Sid certainly could have granted Glen's wish.

But Glen's quest to manage Sid failed. Glen's lever had no fulcrum. Sid was so epically incompetent that he failed to recognize his own incompetence.[33] Sid's self-appraisal was so high that it never crossed his clouded mind that Glen's global support efforts were all that stood between Sid and utter failure. The old fool truly thought that he was doing his job well, and to prove that point, Sid would trot out gushing reviews from the contractors. Sid chose to be blind to the reason the contractors lauded him no end; they all knew that buttering up Sid was a sure-fire route to even more lucre.

Glen's dilemma was worse than that of a two-tailed dog; if he continued to do all of his work and all of Sid's too, Sid's projects would succeed. But that meant the Big Boys would give Sid all the credit and think that Glen was—adequate. And Glen would be screwed. Or, if Glen slacked off and left Sid's work undone, Sid's projects would fail. Sid would blame Glen, and the Big Boys would view Glen as—incompetent. Glen was screwed, no matter what.

---

[33] In the field of psychology, the Dunning—Kruger effect is a cognitive bias in which people of low ability and self-awareness mistakenly assess their cognitive ability as greater than it is.

Lesson 7.2: In order to be managed from below in task performance, the manager must be sufficiently cognizant to realize that he cannot perform his job without the subordinate's help.

Sid was eventually relieved of his command, but in a way that was a grave injustice to Glen. It was not Sid's global incompetence that led to his downfall; his growing dementia took him out instead. The first public display of undeniable dementia took place when Sid bought a chest-full of counterfeit military medals and attempted to impersonate a retired Navy Admiral at a social function attended by numerous retired military officers. Things went from bad to worse soon after, at a grand formal banquet. Sid had a throw-chicken-bones-on-the-floor tantrum because in his opinion, chicken was not a suitable entrée to set before an epicure such as he.

Seeing the dementia as an insoluble problem, the Big Boys hastened to put Sid out to pasture and did not pause to consider the decade or more of demonstrated nonfeasance preceding the proof of dementia. As a result, Glen went unrewarded for his many years of managing his manager so effectively that his manager didn't realize he was being managed.

Lesson 7.3: To succeed in managing your manager, you must have a quid to provide, a pro to leverage your quid, and a clearly defined quo. To successfully leverage your quid, your pro must have functional fulcrum.

Case Study 3: Fred and Donald

Fred was an able manager who had a problem with alcohol. Donald, his number one subordinate, managed Fred and kept him productive and out of trouble for years with the quid of preventing Fred's drinking from bringing him down. Donald did four things for Fred:

a) Donald stayed sober when Fred drank. Donald was the designated driver before there were designated drivers.

b) When it came time for Donald to upgrade his home to a better neighborhood, he searched for and purchased a place a mile farther from work than Fred's house. As a result, Donald could drive Fred home from work or from the airport after they had been out on business travel and it attracted no questions at all.

c) Donald took special care to monitor Fred's written output and attend meetings in place of Fred when there was evidence of binge drinking, when Fred was in post-vacation recovery, or at times of high tension.

d) Donald made a concerted effort to collaborate with Fred while Fred was preparing for key meetings. Donald often came along to these meetings "just tagging along to carry Fred's briefcase — Fred's back is giving him trouble".

This managerial inversion worked very well because Fred valued Donald's aid and if Donald ever exploited his advantage, it was subtle. Donald was never perceived as coveting Fred's job, but that could have been Donald's quo all along; when Fred retired, Donald moved up to fill Fred's shoes with nary a stubbed toe or blister.

Remark: A notable thing about this example is that during the several years that the Donald was managing Fred, things worked out more to the advantage of Fred rather than to the favor of Donald.

Case Study 4: A manage-the-manager conflict

Will was the "Associate Manager" in a DA department with three people; Frank, who was Will's manager, Elizabeth (Lib) Eedoh, who was Frank's administrative assistant (she was most definitely not Will's admin, too), and Will. The department held responsibility for management of Quality Control (QC) for component suppliers.

Frank's predecessor Charlie[34] had devised the sampling schemes for the QC department and Frank had inherited all the sampling setups. Frank didn't know diddly about automation, though, so the system he devised to extract the results from the sampling efforts was barely operational. The resulting QC function was messy and paper-intensive. Stacks of QC reports streamed onto Frank's desk in an unceasing and mind-numbing manner.

After Frank cleverly hired Will, the reports flowed directly onto Will's desk, not pausing for a moment for Frank's review. Will actually read the reports, evaluated the results, and wrote draft memos recommending acceptance or rejection of each of the hundreds of lots of components.

---

[34] Unfortunately, after Charlie set up the sampling plans, he died suddenly. The sampling systems were put in place with Frank as the lead author, not Charlie.

Frank had Lib replace the cover memos on Will's drafts with cover memos bearing Frank's imprimatur. She then sent the memos out under Frank's name. This so streamlined the process for Frank that he had lots of time to work on his bridge game, crosswords, his stock holdings, and to pass the time of day with Lib.

Will was a young man who had recently married a divorcee with three sons, each of whom was a handful. His new wife was a nice enough lady but she couldn't handle the boys, so to get away from them, she worked outside the home at a minimum wage job and then spent all she earned on child care. The boys' father had fled the state to avoid paying child support. Thus, Will had to have a job sufficient to keep a household of five afloat. The DA job paid just barely enough. There were no other QC jobs available in the city.

Will hired on at DA with solid credentials and substantial experience at multiple points on the specifications-testing-acceptance chain. He hit the ground running and had the QC operation humming in a couple months. Soon, after reviewing the relevant job descriptions and summary memos, Will concluded that he was doing all of his job and he alone was also doing virtually all of Frank's job, too. Examination of the archived files together with conversations with Frank's long-term work contacts led Will to further believe that he was doing Frank's job better than Frank ever had.

Frank held considerable autonomy within the company. By contrast, Will held autonomy to the extent that he had his choice of black, dark blue, or deep burgundy ink ball point pens.

Will, Frank, and the economic model

With this for background, let's see how the Will/Frank show plays out using the quid-pro-quo manage-the-manager model.

Will's quid was his ability to do both his job and Frank's job and do it all better than Frank.

Regarding pros, Will had many options. Rumor had it and Will had witnessed Frank's weaknesses for wine, women, and song — and a DWI now and then. Will had documented proof of serious shortfalls in Frank's reporting of testing results prior to Will's hiring. Will suspected that Frank had long since forgotten or never knew how to do most of the tasks required by Frank's job description.

Will's quo was simply being allowed to improve the QC function. He saw how he could streamline some of the processes, automate others, utilize new technology for report generation, and reduce dependency on Lib's often questionable work. At first glance, it seemed there could be no reason to not adopt Will's ideas to bring the QC procedures into the modern era.

Accordingly, Will put together an impressive brochure of available technology, labor-reducing procedures, and simplified processes. He met with Frank. The conversation began as a constructive discussion, but Frank got worried about his job and Lib's, so Frank got defensive.

"If it ain't broke, don't fix it!" Frank snarled, as he attempted to discredit Will's brochure. Under threat of firing for insubordination, Frank ordered Will to leave his office and destroy the brochure.

Dealing with failure

At this point, being just ever so slightly pissed off about Frank's stonewall resistance to efforts to improve productivity and reduce errors, Will decided that he, not Frank, should manage QC. Lib was unneeded and Frank should be assigned an opportunity to dawdle away his days on the golf course rather than behind a desk.

Frank changed his mind, too. Lib had Frank's ear (both ears, actually, and Will guessed other things as well), and work from her desk began showing up on Will's. She made it clear that while a task might fall within her job description, Frank had told her that Will had a lot of free time so he could pick up slack wherever needed. The good news was that maintaining her fingernails was so time-intensive that there was hardly a minute left for finding work for Will.

Will tuned into the rumor mill on the Lib/Frank relationship. This led nowhere; Frank was indeed banging Lib, but Frank's third wife was a competitive woman who had married Frank because other women found Frank attractive, too. She was also a high maintenance lady and way more worried about the loss of Frank's paychecks than the loss of Frank's affections.

There was substantial evidence that Frank had a major drinking problem. But Frank was a little proud about how much alcohol he could put down and still make it to work in the morning. The wrinkle was that Frank's favorite drinking buddy was Frank's boss Norman. The only enabler Frank needed for his drinking habit was a key to the cabinet that held the Famous Grouse, Norman's favored brand of scotch. Frank had history on his side, too. He was the face of Quality Control at DA. Norman made sure of that. Frank had once been a front office toady and had been thrust into the QC slot because the company thought that with Charlie putting the sampling plans in place, Frank couldn't possibly screw it up.

Will had a quid, a plethora of pros, and a quo, but the pros were useless because Will had no fulcrum to leverage his quo. Frank was beneath reproach, so he had no reason to accept Will's management from below.

Will's end run

Will did not destroy the brochure as Frank ordered. In fact, Will had soon assembled convincing evidence of Frank's non-feasance, a far larger problem than Will had imagined. The more Will dug, the worse he found the problem to be — evidence of possible fraud and even bribery. Not only was Frank ignorant of most things in QC, he knew nothing about anything else, either.

By this time, Will had no intention of moving on to a greener pasture. He set out to usurp Frank's job.

Will Will prevail through conventional HR and personnel processes? Nope, Will won't. It's as simple as that. He was up against a two-level management wall[35]. To get to where he wanted to go, he had to make an end run.

Will put up with Frank's nonsense for a few more months, documenting every move he made and every move that Frank should have made. Will took particular care to record passages in Frank's final reports that were "similar" to passages in Will's "preliminary" drafts. It was obvious that Frank's reports were just Will's with different cover sheets and distribution lists. Will assembled a packet of material a good two inches thick. He went to considerable lengths to present a balanced picture, but his attempts to show Frank's viewpoint only made the indictment of Frank more convincing.

But then heads rolled in DA's House of Lords. Frank and Norman now reported to a dreaded hardliner VP who was just transferred over from the Phoenix office.

Will saw no hope for his situation, so he took his first week of vacation in two years to interview for two jobs in El Paso. Will was offered one of the jobs in writing at the close of the interview; the offer was a certainly a step up in job quality, but not a big step up salary-wise, so Will asked for two weeks to decide if he'd accept or decline.

Thinking he had little to lose by talking to the new VP, Will asked for an audience. This was risky, because the VP was two rungs above Norman on the company ladder and jumping rank at DA was regarded as grounds for termination.

---

[35] One can usually work around a single-level management wall, but a two-level wall is just about insurmountable.

The VP didn't even touch Will's package of material before he dressed Will down for not going to Frank.

"Well, actually, I went to Frank. That has been done," Will said, "but Frank ignored my first packet which dealt only with ideas to improve productivity and efficiency. He didn't open it before ordering me to destroy it. Then he declared that I needed more work to do since I had time to put the packet together. This packet contains all the material from the first packet and material elicited from archived records. It shows that Frank has not been performing well."

"Then you should have gone **to Norman** with this!" the VP roared.

"Norman refused to speak with me. His admin warned me, though, that he had directed Frank to take disciplinary action."

"Oh," the VP said, in a testy tone, "and now you want **me,** on your behalf, to jump into this mess that you alone have created? Well, young man, unless I find issues in this document that are very important, I am contacting Norman and Frank myself. You will indeed be looking for a new job."

Will stood, politely thanked the VP, and closed the discussion by saying. "Contact my supervision if you wish. I will not be looking for another job, though, because I have another offer in hand. If you find no merit in my concerns, I plan to accept that offer." With that, Will handed the VP a letter tendering his resignation.

This was nowhere near the level of terror the VP had intended to inflict, so he quietly accepted the resignation letter. Will left the VP's office composing a domestic scene song and dance about how transplanting the boys into a fresh environment in El Paso would make controlling them easier rather than harder.

On Monday morning, Frank announced that he had decided to retire. On Monday afternoon, the VP notified Will that he'd been named as the temporary QC department manager, contingent on approval by Norman's replacement. On Tuesday morning, Lib put in for a transfer.

Lesson 7.4: However egregious they might be, weaknesses in performance are harder to exploit than weaknesses of the flesh. This is because failing performance requires extensive documentation, while assertions of lust have inherent credibility.

Remark: Will succeeded because he was good at his job, willing to work very hard, and to take risks. He needed some good luck, too. Had the senior management not been changed at that crucial moment, Will would have been fired and endured Norman's lifetime emnity in addition to Frank's.

Chapter 8

The Hardest People to Manage

Some guys claim that managing **good** employees is as easy as smiling at a pretty lady. We'd put it about on par with mustering up a smile for a plain lady, but ever striving for conciliation, we'll concur that managing **good, ordinary, productive** workers is easy enough. Beyond this opening compromise, though, finding consensus on easiness spurs more debate than a frat house discussion of sorority girls.

In view of the general lack of agreement on the difficulty in managing employees, we have set out to bring order to the topic. We have developed the 10-point Moh's Scale of Hardness to Manage, so named to honor and commemorate the classic Mohs Scale of Mineral Hardness[36].

At the top of the Moh's Management Scale (Exhibit 3) are the **ordinary workers**. These quiet folks rarely get their due—they work thoughtfully, they do their best most of the time, they do well enough all the time, and they earn their pay. They vary from the joy-to-know-and-supervise to the troops who are doing okay but would do better if you could find them a spot where their skills and persona could flourish. Overall, we think they are the most fun and least difficult to manage. You are blessed if your staffers are of this ilk.

---

[36] Mohs Hardness of Minerals Scale—the classic rock scratch test. See Wikipedia.

Exhibit 3
Moh's Hardness to Manage Scale[37]

Employee	Range of Hardness Scores
Ordinary staff	1.0 (no problems) to 2.1 (square pegs in round holes)
Stars	1.3 (besties) to 5.2 (divas)
Abysmal failures	2.1 (way betters) to 2.5 (worseners)
Antagonists	3.6 (debaters) to 6.0 (debasers)
Obliviati	4.1 (out to lunch) to 6.5 (eaten for lunch)
Marginal improvers	4.4 (slight improvers) to 6.8 (improve just enough to hang on)
Retired-in-place	4.8 (<3 mos to retire) to 8.3 (> 2 yrs to retire)
Misguided over-achievers	7.9 (old, angry) to 16.0 (middle-aged with religious empowerment)

---

[37] The Moh's Hardness to Manage Scale is a work-in-progress device intended to weave whole-cloth nonsense into the fabric of the chaotic workplace.

The next step down on the Moh's Scale are the **stars**. Some want us to think that managing the star employee is always a piece of cake. We don't know about that; even with the easiest-to-manage star you'll need to find a way to retain her when she gets a "once in a lifetime opportunity" offer from a competitor. Since stars vary from the low-maintenance besties to the high-maintenance divas, we are sure of only one thing. You'll be better off with a prima donna instead of divas, because "divas" is plural and "prima donna" is exactly singular. We have found that while managing a prima donna is not easy, simultaneously managing two or more competing divas is damn near impossible.

Just below the stars are the **abysmal failures.** The good news here is that some of these guys are so bad that they are easy; if the guy's failings can be isolated, you might be able to fix him with corrective plans and monitoring systems. If he greatly improves, your life and his will be better. You'll be a hero and he'll not hate you quite so much. Your no-extra-cost added benefit is that if he doesn't shape up, you'll already have the termination evidence in hand so you can quickly arrange for him to ride in another bus.

The next step down on the Hardness Scale are the **antagonistic types.** They are less fun than the failures, but some of the low-end-of-the-scale debaters and questioners are worth serious reclamation efforts. If you can identify the reason(s) for the antagonism(s), it may be possible to actually correct the problem(s) and the rewards for success are often high because these quarrelsome types are usually smart and capable of doing lots of good work. And, for these guys, the downside is okay, too. If you can't resolve the issues that make the antagonistic guy such a pain in the ass, firing him will be satisfying, savage glee for you and likely to bring great joy to all others in your department.

Next on the Moh's Hardness Scale are the **obliviati.** They aren't unhappy, they aren't angry, they aren't militant, and they aren't all that lazy. The best of them are just out to lunch. An employee needs to be good at seeing what needs to be done but the obliviati are blind to task needs. So, as their manager, you have to spend beaucoup painful and unrewarding hours keeping them busy.

These guys get into the system because they are hard to spot during the hiring process. Even a guy who'll eventually get eaten for lunch can blend into the applicant crowd—he'll have okay credentials, he won't piss people off during the job interview, and he's much less likely to raise red flags than the guy with an axe to grind. He'll have an okay-to-good grade point average in school because conformity and a good memory will get a so-so student through a lot of classes. He'll do more or less what he's told to do more or less when he's told to do it. The one sure thing is that unless you tell him what to do, he'll spend his time keeping his nose clean.

And this leads right into the bigger problem. In a bureaucracy, keeping the nose clean is better rewarded than finding a cure for the snotty nose—if you don't screw up, you are rewarded. If you make an error, you get punished. So conventional, safe action that can produce at most a moderate benefit is usually rewarded, while innovative, higher risk action that can produce a huge reward is often punished. Zero risk might be okay on a manufacturing line, but it's not the climate you want for creativity.

Lesson 8.1: If you want innovation and creativity, you will want junior employees and minor managers who are not risk-averse.

Remark: If a junior guy makes a mistake, senior staff or management will likely find it and fix it with minimal loss. If a senior guy screws up, subordinates will be reluctant to point it out, making it likely that the mistake is released into the world. So, it makes sense to encourage a young type to be bold and learn from mistakes, while making the senior guy hold the line on errors. If the senior guy can't hold the error line, replace him with a compulsive senior woman.

We are now getting into the raggedy, pain-inflicting segments of the Scale, the **marginal improvers**. These guys are losers who improve a little but don't improve enough. There is managerial quicksand between the guys who fail to improve properly and the guys who fail to fail properly; these neither/nor guys require individually[38] tailored plans.

---

[38] Individually tailored plans are often referred to as "exit plans".

A step below the marginal improver is the **retired-in-place** employee. In our experience this is almost strictly a guy thing. He knows how to do just enough to keep from getting into trouble. He gets bigger bucks for less productivity than any other segment of the workforce because he usually enjoys unjustified support from a system that values experience over performance.

An example here is the disheartening case of Old Joe, a loser who wasn't good enough when he was young to be a has-been when he got old. We had Joe all primed to go out the door, but then this vacuum-brained kid in HR talked Joe into withdrawing his retirement letter "because the company always needs experienced people".

It's just not worth your effort to try to fix things with guys who have just a year or two to go to retirement, but the guy who has settled into his own little fortress with five to ten years before retirement is a big drag on your staff.

One way to deal with these retired-in-placers (RiPs) is to inflict training and force introduction of new systems. You may have to prematurely obsolete some systems, but it might well be worth the cost and effort to flush out the RiP who has dug in. Another approach is to make the RiP guy report to your just promoted, fire-in-belly, hardnosed junior manager. It will piss off the old guy so he might retire, and for sure the young boss will learn a lot.

At the bottom of the Moh's Scale is the **misguided over-achiever**. This is the guy who'd be a star if he wasn't so committed to doing the wrong thing really, really well.

There may be no human more celebrated than the selfless, dedicated-to-task, over-achiever (OA). He takes on the world single-handedly and wins. It's better than being rich, beautiful, intelligent, or charming. Over-achievers are so laudable and so perfect in all regards that even the utterly out-of-control OA achieves perfection—he's a perfect pain in the ass. These guys can be spectacularly bad; we had one who scored a 16 on a 1 to 10-point scale.

The misguided OA is worthy of examination.

The OAs work harder and get more done, and do it with more opposition and less training, less support, and smaller salary than the mediocre achiever, or the oh-so humble underachiever. What could there ever be about OAs that's not to like?

Um, there's just a thing or two. Such as whether the OA is producing the correct thing? With appropriate quality? At acceptable cost, without excessive resource consumption? While not generating office conflicts? And without driving management nuts?

The misguided OA is really good at what he does, but being good at something isn't always a positive thing in the global sense. For instance, if you live by a lake, you'll find that geese are really good at covering your lawn with turds.

The second big issue with over-achievement is inducing the OA to implement change when change is due. OAs get things done by shutting out distractions so it's hard to catch their attention. While you are trying to get them to listen, their eyes glaze from thinking about how much they could have gotten done if you weren't talking at them.

Particularly, old female OAs supervised by young male managers do not graciously welcome critique. When a young manager who lacks earned stripes crosses swords with a veteran OA, the sword duel soon deteriorates into a pissing match with the young manager on the downwind side. Further, the veteran's peers will see it as a threat to seniority, and right or wrong, they'll tend to ally against the greenhorn. We hasten to add that OAs are no more receptive to peer critique than management critique, however.

There is no question about whether the OA works hard or gets volumes of work done. But the least questionable of all is whether the OA self-identifies as an OVER-ACHIEVER with a glorious work ethic. Waste no time collecting data on how outstanding he is, because he'll already have done the math. Should you want to hear things clearly, try being so bold as to suggest that things could be just a wee bit better if only the OA would read the fricking instructions or follow the damn SOPs (Standard Operating Procedures). Comparisons citing tremendous sacrifice, staggering output, and negligible support will soon pour forth.

And OAs have a lock on halos and benefits of doubt. Terrific productivity overwhelms all shortcomings. But remember — OAs spend their time doing things they deem to be important and if their deem doesn't coincide with management's deem...

Case Study

This case study arose from a federal government costs-plus-10% contract scrounged up by Desert Aromatics in an hour of financial desperation.

The contract, signed some years before the Bernie epoch, covered a spectrum of data management tasks performed on what were probably personnel records of regional workers with classified clearances. Everything was coded and the code keys in the code books were themselves coded, so odds were good that it was entirely nonsense. Bernie was not about to raise this dreaded validity issue, though, because once systems and staff were in place to do the work, supplying these data services was a fine cash cow.

The contract was Fed funded, so US Civil Service pay scales applied. This was a sweet deal for the DA hires because finding local clerical level jobs that paid as well as a GS-5 was nigh impossible—keeping books for the Albuquerque Operations Office of the Medellin Drug Cartel paid a tad more, but that was only one job and it was plagued by recurrent unexplained personnel disappearances.

The contract required preparing simple-minded reports purportedly covering age, training, and clearance status. The reports were presented at oversight meetings held at secure federal facilities. For the code clerks, travel to these meetings was exciting plum duty. Just why anyone would willingly go to Amarillo and spend three days a hundred feet underground in a lead-lined bunker at the Pantex nuclear weapon storage site was mysterious. But, three days underground near Amarillo was no doubt preferable to three days above ground near Amarillo.

In the early days, because everything about the projects was shielded from prying eyes, the fundamental axiom of data management[39] was followed; don't ask, don't tell. Since the staff had nothing to gain by doing things to bias the outcomes and all were paid the same regardless of their work accuracy or quantity, "close enough for government work" was the order of the day. Life was good.

The most senior clerk on the staff was Sylvia; long in the nose and longer still in the tooth. She KNEW her job, and by her reckoning she was very, very good at it. Others supposed she must be pretty good, because she alone handled the biggest project in the contract and all the other projects had two or more clerks. Sylvia often found need to remind Bernie of that. She wasn't quite so outspoken about why things were so, though; she was such a wretched martinet that no assistant clerk had ever lasted more than a week on Sylvia's project.

Sylvia was unique in that she kept her records using the McBee Card System, an 1896 technology that had been obsoleted around the turn of the century[40]. Because the cards-with-punched-holes-in-tabs system was obsolete, McBee Cards were not available through conventional supply channels. Hence, Sylvia had to make do by reusing and patching. As a result, many of her thousands of McBee Cards had a dozen or more patched-in tabs.

---

[39] To prevent finding data errors, prevent looking for data errors.
[40] That's the 20th century, not the 21st.

But her patches fell off and the glue made the cards sticky, and since all her cards were old and groused up on their edges, proper alignment of the cards, tabs, and holes was the exception rather than the rule. All in all, the McBee system held a well-earned place in the Museum of Quaint and Misguided Technology.

So long as there was no pressing need to check her accuracy, things went along swimmingly for Sylvia's McBee system. But there was trouble in paradise. Bernie obtained access to an IBM 1620 and a punch card sorter. The mandate came from above that all contract records were to move onto the computer, so Bernie dumped the whole nine yards onto John's lap. John had to face two big problems immediately:

1. The card sorter was highly sensitive to voltage fluctuations, so it tore up a wad of cards every time the air conditioner kicked on.

2. Getting run time on the 1620 was a several-hour/written-request/justification-needed/suck-up-to-the-1620-administrator task.

But John prevailed and IBM card record keeping came of age. Learning of this, the Fed bean counters demanded that John prove that data quality was maintained. The good news was that data quality could be measured by comparing results from the IBM card system and Sylvia's McBee cards. The bad news was that the McBee and IBM card systems were discrepant like 90% of the time. Fuss, furor, arguments, and antagonisms followed.

The work to rectify the disagreements did help to improve things, though, and over the course of a few months, the ratio of IBM card/McBee errors went from about 1.1/1.0 to about 0.1/1.0. In Sylvia's eyes, IBM's 0.1 was unacceptably high. In John's eyes, Sylvia's 1.0 was unacceptably high. Bernie feared he'd lose his whole herd of cash cows to Taytes, because in his eyes, the 0.1 was high and Sylvia's 1.0 was utterly intolerable. Bernie was onto John like white on rice.

The John/Sylvia interaction became unpleasant. Sylvia cited her remarkable productivity, how hard she worked, and how she alone had kept her project from falling into chaos again and again. She had always been lauded for her overachievements, and now this foolish young man without an ounce of sense or a gram of experience said her work needed to be changed? No, her work was excellent. Her work effort was unparalleled. Her work was the standard by which others' work should be judged. She alone could read the McBee cards, only she could find answers from them, and the McBee counts had always been good enough.

Sylvia duly recorded all of her concerns and forwarded them to HR. HR ignored her, because Bernie was leaning all over HR and HR cared about people, not processes.

John ordered Sylvia to stop using the McBee cards and to support only the IBM card processes. Not surprisingly, she balked until Bernie stepped in and he, too, ordered Sylvia to comply. She was not about to be insubordinate to Bernie. He'd been a manager almost as long as Sylvia had been a clerk, and besides, they were both from New York. Bernie was from Queens and she was from Staten Island.

Thinking Bernie had solved his problem, John went back to other tasks—until the next summary report for the project was issued. The morning after the IBM card-based report was released for internal review, Sylvia appeared at John's door, gloating. There were nine errors in his report, she declared. John investigated and found that she was wrong about seven of the alleged errors, but two were real keypunch errors. Two errors were two too many.

John was baffled. Sylvia did not know how to run the card sorter. Surely it would have taken her a month to go back through her entire file of source documents. How in Hellerith did she find the two errors?

Easy. Sylvia smugly explained that she had used the McBee cards. She had been maintaining the McBee cards on the QT, working nights and weekends.

She was proud to the point of ecstasy about finding the two errors—so proud that the Tale of Two Errors was burned into the organization's clerical folklore that very day. That she had blithely ignored her direct supervisor's order to use only the IBM card system was not a concern. The McBee card system had been vindicated! And it was to be preferred because of system experience and supervisory inexperience. That Sylvia had made 7 errors with her McBee cards mattered not a whit. John lost, badly.

Lesson 8.2: It took only two stinking errors to sink John. With a new system, you need zero errors to prevail in a conflict with an errant over-achiever.

Under the rules of US Civil Service, John was unable to do anything meaningful to resolve the conflict except to complain upstairs. So he did. Bernie threw up his hands and told John to live with it. The cost of fixing the problem exceeded the cost of the problem.

Amazingly, though, Bernie himself fixed things six months later. When contract renewal time came, Bernie called Taytes and negotiated a trade of Sylvia's project for a troubled Taytes project. The project Taytes turned over was IBM card based and had no node where McBee cards could be squeezed in without compromising all previous work and records. Sylvia chafed in this new assignment and took retirement within a year.

Sylvia's OA issues

1. Sylvia indeed put her all into her job. Being unmarried and apparently having almost no life outside her work, she existed for kudos and was willing to work night and day to keep the kudos coming.

2. Sylvia treasured her system and the control she had over it, but her system had become more important to her than the product of her system.

3. After Sylvia had retired and all the shouting was done, John reflected that if Sylvia had been convinced that God was on her side, too, she would have been utterly impossible to manage.

General misguided OA issues

1. In the usual case, the entrenched misguided OA has developed the processes that are under fire. The processes are extensions of the OA's being and his first thoughts are to flatly reject change because the process is already perfect.
2. Bailiwicks get established by rejecting outside input. "Exemplary" workers are rarely eager to hear of flaws or of ways to improve.
3. Often, the only practical solution is to redirect the misguided OA into a totally changed assignment.

But what about over-achieving leaders?

1. "Leaders" are OAs. They step up and take charge. But are they leading in the right direction? Leading in the wrong direction preempts going in the right direction, so not leading beats leading in the wrong direction.

2. The act of stepping up to take charge uses one sector of the brain. Understanding what's going on utilizes a different sector. These sectors may be disconnected.

3. But if you challenge someone who has stepped up to take charge, you damn well better have a plan and know how to make your plan happen.

Lesson 8.3: Do not mistake accomplishment for intelligence.

Chapter 9

The Bartender Management Model

Let us consider the bartender. This is a person (usually male, but of course some of the very best are female) who ends up wearing the white hat no matter what goes wrong. It's been that way since the beginning of time, too. You want proof? Jesus cut his teeth on miracles as the master bartender at Cana. And who ever heard a "Two guys walk into a bar" joke where the bartender turns out to be the obtuse jerk? It's unlikely that there even was such a joke, but if there ever was one, it sure as hell wasn't funny.

But what does the bartender do that is of management interest? For us it matters not a whit if he charges for Black Jack Daniels while pouring shorted shots of Jack Daniels Green. We want to know how our bartender interacts one-on-one with a loner who comes in bearing woes and tribulations and spends the evening telling the bartender how things really are[41].

Here's how it might go: After a couple drinks our bartender and the loner strike up a conversation. Bartenders are really good at striking up conversations with loners.

---

[41] Sure, the drunkster's view will feature alternative facts, will probably be intentionally misleading, and possibly dishonest, but there's always plenty of words. It's like what's in political campaign speeches.

A drink or two later, the loner reveals that he's not totally thrilled by how things are going at work. With his booze-loosened tongue, he laments. He fears his situation is hopeless. Although he doesn't know the bartender from Jack Schmitt's gray stud horse, the loner unloads anyway. The loner shares his thoughts, real and imagined threats, and inner aspirations. Every flaw in his work environment is detailed. The loner says things never spoken to anyone else and speaks of thoughts never thought before, at least during daylight hours.

All the while, our good bartender is a model of empathy. He seems to listen attentively but somehow keeps his apron spotless. He never acts surprised by what the loner says, for our bartender must convey an image of having heard it all. He grunts a lot and says "um" now and then. He eventually offers generic words of solace and succor, some of which might be taken for wisdom. When the loner starts having trouble clinging to the barstool, our bartender calls Uber on behalf of the loner.

The loner and our bartender part as comrades and dearest of friends. Our bartender pockets the tip, which may be large. But the biggest tips are still way less than a half hour on a shrink's couch and we'd err badly by not recognizing that our bartender has rendered a valuable counseling and guidance service.

But does this counseling and guidance have lasting influence, or is our bartender just listening to a drunk unload, knowing nothing will be changed in the morning? It depends. On occasions[42], bartenders do exert considerable influence over the actions of their patrons, but not all bartenders are influential and not all their influences are positive. Why? Let's take a look at this:

What does the influential bartender have going?

A. Common sense

Good bartenders' best customers believe their bartenders are uncommonly blessed with common sense. Considering the clientele, this is hardly surprising.

Joe Sixpack, a "common sense" working stiff guy comes into the bar laden with woes. The only way Joe can view his miseries is through his mind's lens of common sense. For Joe, the only tenable explanation for his tormenters' behaviors is their lack of common sense.

Joe downs a couple. The only available ear is attached to Mac, a friendly bartender, so Joe sets to bending it. Mac listens in an empathetic manner while Joe bares his litany of grievances. As the night wears on and Joe downs a couple more, the concept of common sense becomes more and more appealing to a man like Joe.

---

[42] Granted, most of these occasions will occur during times of patrons' elevated blood alcohol levels.

All of Joe's woes are rooted in simple common sense. As Joe's tab grows, Mac disputes fewer and fewer of Joe's multitude of claims of injustice. Joe can't tell if Mac knows his ass from his elbow, but the more Mac agrees with him, the more Joe becomes convinced that Mac values common sense. That's proof that Mac has common sense. And a lot of it.

The ambiance further enhances the bartenders' reputations of having common sense; they are operating on their home turf, doing their things on their own schedule, and they quickly learn to keep their mouths shut until they've had time to read the situation unfolding before them.

B. A Common Law Shrink's Certificate[43]

Mac, the successful and influential bartender, functions as a poor man's psychologist. He subtly pries out information without seeming to pry and then, like a fortune teller, uses this information to tailor generic advice.

And, of course, when the bartender throws in one or two folksy Dr. Phil style stock phrases like "The dog don't hunt", "Sometimes you just got to give yourself what you wish someone else would give you", or "Hey, buddy, I hear ya" he'll go a long way toward comforting the wretched drunkster.

---

[43] The Common Law Shrink's Certificates are awarded in covert ceremony to the top 10% of the class on the last day of training at accredited schools of bartending. It's one of these secret handshake and password things.

C. A non-judgmental viewpoint

Okay, we really mean selectively non-judgmental. Mac, the influential bartender never ever blames Joe for Joe's drunken dilemmas. No matter what. Joe's boss, Joe's wife, Joe's girlfriend, Joe's barber, and Alphie, that asshole bouncer at the place across the street, are all appropriate targets for blame, but Joe never causes nor owns the problems.

Problem ownership is an accountability that sober people are just going to have to accept. Drunks have more than enough difficulty with the problems they don't own.

D. Language skills

Mac, the influential bartender, will possess selective listening skills, together with a working command of the barstool vernacular. This will allow Mac to instinctively know which words to heed among Joe Sixpack's complaints, and Mac will excel at validating these complaints with words of wisdom that slip seamlessly into the conversation. Should Mac utilize Joe's territorial patois as well, Joe will grasp, admire, and even come to embrace Mac's every utterance.

E. The crux

And this brings us to the choke point in the drunkster and bartender interchange. What the bartender says must sound enough like sense to be taken as sensible by the variably (i.e., semi-to-totally) drunk dude. The truly influential bartender knows how to work through this maze — what sounds sensible to an intelligent, sober man has little to do with what makes sense to the dude who has already downed two or four beers and was but so clever when he stepped in the door.

But just mastering the language is not enough. As in social work, where the social worker deals with drug abuse, educational level, racism, socioeconomic status, and funding, the bartender needs to skillfully navigate the complex interactions of degree of drunkenness versus intellect versus inner redneck versus station in life versus how big the tip will be.

Successful drunkster manipulation requires the bartender to master the Goldilocks challenge; not too little booze and not too much booze, warnings and cautions spoken not too soon and not too late, and common-sense wisdom neither understated nor overstated.

There's timing, too – suggestions offered after a single drink might be brushed aside, but these ideas may well be embraced after three drinks have cast a rosy glow on the matters of the day. But should these exact same words be uttered after the sot has doubled down his game from morose to bellicose, the words may be taken as an insult or challenge, and crash headlong into a wall of suspicion.

It's clear that the bartender must tread carefully, because errors that put the tip at hazard are everywhere.

The bartender strategy of management

Is there any such thing as a bartender's approach to management? If there isn't, surely there is a place for something derived from it. As a result of listening to guys' tales of woe, bartenders may have greater access to workers' complaints than any other segment of society. There simply has to be some managerial application[44] for all this information.

Wouldn't it be swell if the subordinate would bare his soul to his manager, and the manager, persuasive as a skilful bartender, could then set the subordinate on the road to complete success?

Just imagine! In but a single meeting, the manager sows the seeds of commitment to company methods, to sanctioned concepts, and to ever-higher goals. These seeds take root in an instant and soon flourish. The workplace becomes a purring machine, productivity soars, and everybody becomes so happy! Careers blossom, vast profits are made, and management is nirvana.

Most bar patrons claim[45] that they clearly understand that bartenders are just observers of human nature who know little of the factual side of the patrons' problems. However, bartenders' opinions and suggestions are still avidly sought and treasured above all else.

---

[44] Any time when you have this much horse shit, there's just gotta be a pony around somewhere.
[45] And most of the patrons do actually understand this, at least early in the evening, anyway.

Just think of how much more highly prized the manager's suggestions should be, because the manager would actually understand the problems and be able to offer carefully thought out solutions to the many issues! The rewards would be staggering.

It's time to glean further understanding and seek operational strategy from a case study.

Case Study

Bernie's first foray into accessing the privileged communications between a bartender and patron was driven by a potentially huge concern; one of DA's network of local spies saw Willie Leake, a senior engineer in Lawrence's section, in furtive discussion with a visiting General Accounting Office (GAO) weenie. This meeting was code red suspicious because it was at a way-off-company dive where everybody went when they didn't want to be seen. (Which was the reason the spy saw Willie; the spy was out with another guy's wife.) The spy dared not step closer to eavesdrop on Willie's conversation, but even without words, the circumstances spoke too loudly. Willie had whistle blowing on the brain.

Bernie did an immediate midnight oil review of Willie's dirty laundry basket. It looked bad. Willie had been a major player on a ton of contracts that were compromised in one or more ways. There was a whole pile of unlaundered undies still bearing the basic brown streak! Everywhere Bernie looked he saw corner-cutting compromises that could turn ugly. The worst were squarely in the midst of the big White Sands project, a contract that was already hanging on the edge of cancellation because of cost overruns and Bernie's expense report padding. Without the White Sands ATM, Bernie's entire empire was suddenly at hazard!

Although Willie was a pretty good engineer, he was already deemed not completely trustworthy because he was prone to mindlessly telling the truth instead of mindlessly reciting the official company line. Further, Bernie's domestic spy reported that Willie's wife had left him for another woman and that Willie's stock holdings had crashed as a result of a flare-up in the Middle East. And with this, there was the no-surprise rumor that Willie had been hitting the bottle in the past few weeks.

The GAO guy had gone back to Washington but was scheduled for another visit in a month. Bernie sprang into action. Claiming national security at stake and calling in a chit from the local FBI guy, Bernie got a tap running on Willie's home phone. That turned up nada in or out with the GAO guy, though.

Intro the bartender

Bernie's next step was to follow up on the drinking report. Willie's favorite watering hole was the Lariat Bar. He'd been seen bending the ear of Jake, the grizzled late-shift head bartender.

Bernie set out to access what Jake knew and then use that information to ward off a likely career-ending GAO investigation and inquisition.

Emulate the bartender

Bernie thought he'd have Lawrence be a Jake—just listen carefully and be empathetic and agreeable while giving Willie the old prime and pump routine.

But Lawrence's only prime and pump venue was a wine and cheese soiree. There was no way in hell that a semi-sober Willie would unload woes onto Lawrence in the evening when he was sure that Lawrence would not respect him in the morning[46]. So, when Lawrence did try the prime and pump, all he heard were the same vague and unresolvable gripes heard at the last performance review. Only fools and tools with nothing to lose speak openly in the presence of their management.

---

[46] Lawrence would really disrespect him in the morning and fire his ass.

Induce the bartender to share data

Bernie's next step was to send a trusted agent, his sister's young masseur, to the Lariat to feel out Jake. But Jake sized up[47] the masseur way quicker than the masseur sized up Jake, and Jake turned into a high-priced clam.

All the $100 bill bought was an admission that a guy who looked a little like Willie came in "once in a while". And the too-big tip was a serious error, too; all it accomplished was to put Jake into his alert[48] mode about Willie.

Lesson 9.1: Never send a boy to do a woman's job.

Bernie figured, and rightly so, that it might be easier for a woman than a man to listen in on Willie and Jake.

The woman had to be not-so-very-attractive and have good hearing. Della's younger sister Louise filled the specs perfectly. When she found out Bernie wanted an unattractive woman, she became eager to run up a tab on Bernie's dime.

Things got messy fast—by the time Willie had downed a couple and noticed Louise hovering nearby, Louise was looking 15 years younger, her teeth had gotten whiter, and her boobs had grown. So, Willie picked her up. Or maybe Louise picked up Willie.

---

[47] Bartenders get really good at sizing up guys. Gotta be careful!
[48] Jake's alert mode—Jake now knew that Willie's woes were worth some serious bucks to somebody.

In any case, Louise later confided with Della that even though she knew from the beginning that it was just a one-night stand, Willie was the sweetest man she had met in years. Which was all true, of course; Willie had his good points and Louise was to the point in life when she got damned few offers.

Lesson 9.2: (Corollary to Lesson 2.1) To make it happen with a bartender, spend some money. Buy the bartender.

By this time, Jake had things pretty well figured out, so he did some digging and got Bernie's name and phone number. A working meeting followed. Jake knew that Willie had put his bundle of evidence in a strong box at a certain branch of the Bank of New Mexico. The little gem of information cost Bernie $2500. When confronted with that knowledge and the threat of the FBI seizing the strong box contents and giving him a one-way ticket to Leavenworth on a trumped-up Espionage Act charge of deliberate mishandling of classified information, Willie repented.

In the end, Willie was quietly transferred to the Phoenix office of DA. Bernie eluded the wrath of the GAO and was eventually able to say his money was well spent[49], besides. Jake would have taken a hit if word of his selling info got out, so Jake's tariff was cheap at twice the price.

---

[49] Bernie's criterion for well spent money—all dollars that he spent that are subsequently recoverable by padding his expense vouchers

Summary

We haven't come up with a scenario that explicitly uses the bartender's approach to management problem solving, but depending on the information quality, there surely could be a place for the information that a bartender can access. Management just has to figure out how to access the bartender.

No matter how much information you can garner from your problem employee's bartender, you ain't gonna reverse 20 years-worth of bad habits all at once. The bartender might help you uncover a particular thorn in the employee's paw that you can remove, though.

Experience indicates that bartenders are a canny lot, so the only sure way to access the bartender's wealth in knowledge is to increase the bartender's wealth in lucre. And don't try to do it on the cheap—you might get the first tidbits at low cost, but the bartender will either want to go onto a retainer or collect substantial tips before the critical mass of information is shared. The bartender is going to demand a high level of confidentiality—if the word gets out that he's selling feedback to his patrons' managements, his tips, his access to information, and his very career will dry to dust.

Chapter 10

Selection of Travel Companions

A significant aspect of management is how you handle things outside of the office. Take travel, for instance. Granted, your travel companions are usually determined *a priori* by project staffing, but there are things you can control, such as choosing a seat on the plane that's far from the individual you're trying to avoid, or taking a later flight, or maybe choosing a different hotel, or even claiming dietary restrictions that force you to forgo group meals.

But before you take steps to modify your travel plans, you need to put some wisdom into choices of traveling companions. Sure, it's nice to fantasize about traveling with attractive, fun-loving members of the opposite sex, but that's rarely an option and even when it is, such trips have high multidimensional hazard rates, with lots and lots of ways to reach regretful endings.

Mostly, though, you need to think about more practical considerations, such as whether Dewey is finally going to start ponying up for cabs, is Paul going to get hit by a pickpocket again and force everyone else to chip in to pay his way, will Jane be on another one of her kicks and shame us into joining her at an oxygen bar rather than in the hotel lounge, or will you have to carry Marshall out of the bar and up to his room and then go bail Jim out again?

Case Study

Work with a cross-functional team of keen professional talents will sometimes result in surprising personality clashes or unexpected synergies. Even though the guy is loathe-worthy, his companionship may be of value. Take, for example, John's old acquaintance, the DA alpha shrink and business cover man, Richard Eastman, MD, ASCP, F(H)AAOA[50].

The man on the street more or less expects a few MDs to be ever so slightly arrogant, but with his charming ways of dealing with laypersons on the team, Eastman stood out from the crowd. For him, a layperson was any fellow worker who:

    a) Was a not unattractive woman who could be laid, or

    b) Was not an MD, or

    c) Did not outrank him on the org chart.

Not to suggest for a moment that he had no social skills, though — if there were women or other MDs about, he liked to be convivial. He hated to say "I this" or "I that" all the time, so he spoke of himself in the third person, calling himself "Big Dick" while enthralling all with tales of his unending spell-shaking and earth-binding accomplishments.

John might have handled this with more aplomb had the doctor not tried to be cutesy — Eastman was forever calling just before lunch to tell John to do a task with a completion deadline of just after lunch on the day before tomorrow.

---

[50] Doctor of Medicine, American Society of Clinical Psychiatrists and Honorary Fellow of the American Amalgamation of Obnoxious Assholes.

John had to give Eastman credit, though—there was never a man who gave John more opportunities to become a better person. Scarcely a day went by when Eastman didn't give John a chance to practice forbearance, understanding, and forgiving. In testimony to the profound regard the support staff held for Eastman, in addition to always addressing him (as he insisted) as "Doctor Eastman" in his presence, in his absence all but a few added the honorary prefix "The" to his self-chosen third person title "Big Dick".

Admiration of The Big Dick had no bounds. Well, for sure there wasn't a limit on the lower end of the admiration scale. It is correct to conclude that Doctor Eastman just wasn't the kind of guy you'd put in charge of saving your bacon.

By now, the reader might doubt that The Big Dick was anyone's most favorite colleague. The short answer is "you guessed it". However, "favorite colleague" and "favorable travel companions" are not equivalent terms. On a trip to Edmonton he turned out to be a boon traveling companion.

The Big Dick led a group to Edmonton for a meeting on the afternoon of December 23rd. Since the party was going out of the US, a full accompaniment was in order; besides The Big Dick, the party included Bullet Bob (a senior manager from Weapons), Patoo Patel (who was probably a lawyer and surely CIA—the US equivalent of a Russian KGB oversight type), Phil the project physicist, and John. Phil and John were bottom rungers because they were actually working on the project, so Phil and John got to carry the handouts for the meeting. That was okay. After the briefcases were stuffed with peripherals there was only one 24-pound box of Xerox paper apiece.

What wasn't so okay was everything else about the meeting.

The Canadian professor asked to meet in early November. Ignoring that the professor was Jewish and thinking that he'd be so eager to leave for the holiday that he'd be a pushover in negotiations, The Big Dick stalled until December 23rd.

The professor was misled into believing that DA's business was making fragrances and dusting powders. His testing device used compressed air to explode foil packets containing tiny bits of silicon, so he thought DA's interest was in dusting powder dispersion. Phil's (and DA's) real interest in the study was learning how the silicon bits dispersed, and using that knowledge to estimate how chunks of shrapnel from tunnel grenades would scatter.

The proclaimed trip purpose was "to review collected study data". The original contract covered only data on where the silicon scattered. When Phil realized that for shrapnel, where the silicon scattered was much less important than how the silicon scattered, he asked the professor to add recording of the silicon flight paths as X-Ray images. However, the X-Ray recording step and X-Ray data were never formally added to the contract. So, the real meeting purpose was to browbeat the professor into giving DA exclusive access to the study data plus the X-Ray tracings and data. And, to do it all for the non-adjusted-for-inflation sum specified in the 3-year-old original budget.

The DA team finally gave the professor three times the original contract sum to complete it all and relinquish rights to all the data. The DA team celebrated the success with a fine self-congratulatory supper of Canadian beef.

But freezing fog rolled in. The drive to the airport on that Christmas Eve morning foretold of drama. The 8:00 AM Northworst direct flight to Chicago was canceled because the aircraft was to be the red-eye coming from Anchorage and the fog at Anchorage was so tight that even the take-offs had been canceled. The fine folks at Northworst wanted the team to stay in Edmonton on the outside chance that if their 1:20 PM flight from Minneapolis could land, the team could be on the 4:15 return flight to Minneapolis.

But an Air Canada plane was already on the ground at Edmonton, so switching to the 8:40 AM Air Canada flight to Winnipeg and connecting with the 1:15 PM Northworst plane to Chicago seemed a way better plan. In June, it might have actually been the better plan. In December, though, there was a de-icing delay. And then the plane sat so long on the taxi strip that it had to be de-iced again. The Air Canada plane was somewhere over Saskatchewan when the 1:15 PM Northworst flight departed from Winnipeg.

The Winnipeg airport was full of Christmas travelers and the only hope was the 6:30 PM Northworst flight to Chicago. It didn't look good—the plane was a short DC-9 with 120 seats and a roster of 123 sold and confirmed reservations.

To make things worse, The Big Dick entered into holy acrimony with the lady at the Northworst help desk. When she finally put the DA names onto the standby list, John's name had dropped to from a potential 8th to 23rd.

It was beginning to look a lot like Christmas in Winnipeg. But, with slim hopes on standby being better than none, it was a relaxing afternoon at the airport. John checked to see what was playing at the airport theater. He'd seen just one movie in the previous six months. Bingo! It was playing. Drifting over to the duty-free store, he was pondering the economics of trying to sneak a jar of the good stuff through customs when he heard gales of coarse laughter coming from the bar.

The Big Dick had found diversion.

The Big Dick greeted John with a hearty, "Have a drink! We'll put this round on your credit card!" and then went back to thrilling the troops with tales of his miraculous deeds and triumphs. He tossed down his drink and called, "Have another! Put it on Phil's card. Ken'll cover it — so have a double!" Ken was Phil's boss, and famed for springing for nothing beyond in-flight bags of peanuts.

By the 4th round of drinks, The Big Dick moved on to how at the U of Colorado he'd been an All Big 8 tight end. Or it might have been All Big 8 Ball, but for sure he'd rocketed to even greater stardom as the team doctor after med school. The bar was awash with tales of The Big Dick's single-handed defeats of legions of evil. Eyes glazed. Patoo dozed off. His stool tipped. A burr on a screw head on the stool's back cushion snagged the sleeve of The Big Dick's plaid, double knit polyester suit coat.

It was a huge, ugly, awful snag. Patoo began to apologize and fret about fixing the problem, but The Big Dick uttered not a word of dismay. He looked down at Patoo, put his hand on Patoo's shoulder in a gesture of noble forgiveness, and then gazed about with a calm and collected demeanor, as if to say, "This is not a problem. Compared to the Herculean perils Big Dick Eastman has vanquished in his long, illustrious, and exciting career, this counts for not even so much as the tiniest bump in the road."

The Big Dick coolly whipped out his cigarette lighter and, in a trice, set fire to the offending loop. The snag flared up with a dense puff of smoke. Quicker than an auctioneer could say, "You damned fool! You're going get us all arrested as American subversives, create an international incident, and burn down the air terminal!" all that remained of the snag was a shiny brown dot. The dot could scarcely be seen against the umber on beige and chartreuse of the plaid suit. A flaming success it was, indeed.

All were taken by his élan. Even the bartender was smitten. By the time the fire extinguisher was back beneath the cash register and the bar fly three stools down had fanned the air, the crowd realized that The Big Dick had led them to the threshold of a whole new form of barroom entertainment.

The Big Dick's suit was cheesy and in its declining years, so the two-inch loop he'd burned off his sleeve was merely the newest of a couple dozen snags on the lower left sleeve. The fronts of his pants legs were all nubby with those errant loops of polyester. The Big Dick was in fact a beefy guy—he was maybe 6'2" and wide bodied, so with the paunch, he weighed in at way better than 250. With about a half-acre of plaid knit suit, there must have been a couple hundred snags to be found.

The Big Dick's cigarette lighter was one of these butane jobs that works like a tiny little blowtorch, and every time he flicked the lighter, a fine pointy blue flame popped out and then a puff of smoke shot up from a loop on the suit.

In no time there was a crowd built up around him, drinking to his latest move and exhorting him to torch this loop or that snag. When one in the crowd insisted that he try to burn the really big one off the back of his collar, The Big Dick borrowed the bar fly's compact mirror and with but a glance in the back-bar mirror, Poof! went the snag amid thundering applause. The hair on the back of his neck was singed, but the snag was no more.

Two more bartenders rushed in from the Air Canada wing of the airport. One just took the drink orders, while the other, an austere older man, placed a huge CO_2 extinguisher on the bar right next to The Big Dick. Decorum would be followed, he said, and safety maintained above all else. The fire extinguisher was on the bar maybe five minutes; it looked impressive but proved a major obstacle as the four bartenders scrambled to fill the mounting calls for drinks. Side bets were placed as to when the whole suit would catch fire, and 3 to 5 said if that happened, the bartender with the moustache wouldn't use the big extinguisher at all. Instead, he'd stimulate sales by exhorting the patrons to douse the flaming suit with their beers.

Above all, frolic flowed. Canadians are better at having fun than we somber Americans, and drunken Canadians have the most fun of all. What had been an uptight crowd of businessmen trying every means to get home for the holiday turned into a joyous festival. Everyone in the terminal came to get in on the fun and excitement! The party swelled as the aircrews, the janitors, and even some Hutterite kids appeared to watch the crazy American torch his suit. Somebody put **Smoke Gets in Your Eyes** onto the piped-in music.

The Big Dick so delighted the crowd that one of the bartenders actually turned down the sound on the taped replay hockey game on the TV. (True, it was only the Bruins demolishing the Maple Leafs, but hey, this was Winnipeg, and Hawkey is not merely the lifeblood of society in The Great White North, it's IMPORTANT to those folks.)

A few minutes later a suit with an earpiece and another suit with one of those little walkie-talkie things appeared. They watched for a bit and then left quietly. Somebody challenged The Big Dick to balance on one foot, put the other leg up on a stool, and using the bar fly's mirror, to take a snag off the back of the raised pants leg. But even as the side bets were going down, the squawk box announced that Northworst Flight 367 to Chicago standby passengers Eastman, Patel, Piper, Phillips, and Smith were to report to gate C-9 IMMEDIATELY. This was special because it was only a quarter after four, boarding wasn't to start for nearly two hours, and standby passengers usually don't hear anything until ten minutes before departure.

Dutifully, The Big Dick pocketed his torch and the DA team trundled off toward the gate. The guy with the earpiece followed, and three or four security guys appeared along with the gate clerk. The gate clerk pulled up the standby list, carefully drew lines through the top eighteen names, and asked the DA people to gather around.

The world has come to expect that Canadians will be civilized and reasonable people, but the gate clerk was almost courtly as he explained how the DA guys could have seats to Chicago if they'd relinquish their tickets in exchange for boarding passes, get on this plane, and take their assigned seats. RIGHT AWAY. If anyone chose to not load right away, or not remain seated in his assigned seat, the agent could not assure there would be a seat to Chicago until the 6:25 AM flight on the first Saturday after New Year. Not a single word was uttered about pressing criminal charges.

Well, the DA guys took their seats. And they remained seated. The rest of the passengers began boarding at 6:15. Every seat on the plane was taken, so it's very likely that every other standby passenger was given the opportunity to spend Christmas Eve in Winnipeg. And, judging from the abusive language heard from the boarding tube just before departure, at least a couple confirmed passengers had the opportunity to extend their visit in The Great White North, as well.

The DA guys got to Chicago almost on schedule, and they caught the last flight to Albuquerque that evening. John could only thank The Big Dick for managing everything in such a way that people truly cared about his traveling needs, and to Winnipeg Airport Security and to Northworst Airlines for finding a way to help.

Lesson 10.1: John's only chances for a less interesting trip were a couple could haves.

Remark: John knew The Big Dick was going to be a pain, so John could have made his move earlier. He could have:
- Pleaded illness or food poisoning to skip the big supper and taken the evening flight home on the 23rd.
- Claimed need to travel earlier and hence separately in anticipation of delays due to taking "necessary" computer equipment along. Any technology-intensive excuse would have worked, though, because The Big Dick understood no technology and disdained all of it.

Chapter 11

Humor in the Workplace

The goal of this chapter is to cast some darkness upon managerial use of humor. Since most attempts to manage humor lack focus, we'll start with a broad brush.

But first, why would you want to bother with humor at all? Some managers hardly ever break a smile and do just fine, e.g., Bill Belichick. Is life without laughs worth living, though? Not for us. Humor in the workplace is a powerful tool that can buoy spirits in bad times, boost productivity, improve work quality, piss people off, depress spirits, and foment rebellion. As a management tool, humor is too powerful to ignore and too useful to not use.

But beware! Some take pride in finding something offensive in every joke they hear and have mastered the art of finding evidence that your ever-pathetic humor attempts insult them, their friends, and their beliefs.

What do we know?

Although it's beyond our reach to define what is funny, in our opinion, a joke needs to have some basis in truth to be funny for more than an instant. Further, the best jokes carry some sort of insight on the state of humanoids. A mere perversity in the environment doesn't cut it.

The spectrum of management of humor in the workplace ranges from you-let-it-happen to you-make-it-happen.

Translated into actions, humor management ranges from posting a bulletin board sign saying, "Let's have more fun around here!" to bringing in Izzy Gesell's[51] humor training course. Somewhere in between is arranging for funny things to occur. Arranging fun is the best and hardest hard way to go.

The winner of the humor game is not the guy who dies after telling the most jokes—or sanctioning the most jokes. Condoning a "joking" atmosphere in the office requires no skill and has the huge advantage that when things turn sour, the manager can point fingers at the guys who have uttered the wrong words or done the wrong things. This works, but badly; practical jokes are usually a problem for everybody except the jerk playing the joke, inoffensive jokes tend to be more offensive than funny, weak jokes aren't worth their air tune, and reaching for laughs deserves a special scorn. And finally, a bullying jerk having "fun" with someone on the staff who is already pissed off can turn into an UGLY situation with lasting repercussions for all hands.

Standing back and letting humor happen is easy and takes no forethought. But handing a free rein to the guy with an ugly sense of humor ensures that one day (i.e., soon) the manager will have to deal with downstream damage control work.

The good thing about humor is that we are all unique. The bad thing about humor is that we are all unique. Almost

---

[51] Izzy Gesell can be found on the web.

anything will be funny for some, but nothing is funny for everyone and very little humor is thought to be funny by almost everyone. This is as it is; some people have narrow views of what is funny. The ultra-serious do not value humor and tolerate only their own sarcasm. A far worse problem is that there live among us the wretched souls who can extract fun and pleasure only from others' pains and sufferings.

You can get some things done by just doing them, though

Are there rules for controlling humor enough to turn it into a management tool? We know that mixing rules with tools and fools makes good rhymes but bad reasons, so we'll skip the rules, throw caution aside, and plunge ahead.

What sorts of things have turned humor into management tools?

The word game

One useful method to teach and at the same time entertain the group at a meeting is the in-depth examination of a term relevant to the purpose of the meeting. Even in the presence of merriment, the relevant term provides a tie line back to the meeting's purpose.

Graphics can help with audience participation, but the graphics need to be carefully thought out. Simple can be effective, as in the following:

Bernie's company was negotiating with a French company. As always, the French had healthy skepticism and demanded a preliminary meeting to assess DA staff's understanding of "French culture". This led, of course, to understanding French phraseology, for in French culture, their language is everything. At least right after sex and wine, language is everything. Well, okay, right after sex, wine, and fine food, language is everything.

John was the only DA guy who knew any French that did not require pardoning before uttering, so Bernie named him as the DA lightning rod. At the preliminary meeting, the lead French guy Henri laid French management terminology onto the DA management team and senior staff.

In script letters, Henri wrote *"raison d'etre"* on his easel, stating the term was useful to describe company missions.

John wrote "reason for being" on his easel. Then he crossed it out, wrote "most important reason for existence" and sat down, just a little pleased with himself.

Henri gave John only a C, though. John had done okay, but as a terminology exercise *raison d'etre* was too easy. "Eet lacks nuance," Henri declared.

Henri's next management word on his easel was *"savoir faire"*. He noted the term had an elusive meaning and must never be translated literally.

John, the quintessential American, violated the no-literal-translation rule, writing "savoir faire = know how".

Henri threw up his hands in disgust. "Mais non! Eet ees much difference from zat! Eet ees like cool — expertise, but wis élan and panache! I geeve you example:

Alphonse comes home from work early one afternoon.

He goes to zee boudoir to change hees clothes, only to

find hees wife Marie in bed wis his best friend Gaston. Alphonse surveys zee situation, and says, 'Continué, s'il vous plait'."

Thinking he understood, John blurted out, "Now I've got it! Alphonse has savoir faire!"

"Mais non!" cried Henri. "Eef Gaston **can** continue, **he** has savoir faire."

Telling the private joke

Suppose you want to share a joke with a few carefully chosen members of your staff. This will usually serve to tighten your inner circle and build comradery, but the joke has to be appropriate and remember the cardinal rule for telling jokes — no matter what, you have to nail the punchline. As in the following example:

Five old friends from university days chanced to meet at a cocktail party at a professional meeting in Atlanta. They were Tony, once a professor who had just started working at a government regulatory agency[52], and four of his former students who were now employed in that regulated industry. The old friends greeted each other warmly and then one of the guys asked Tony how it was to work for his new leader "Boss", a man well known to all in the industry as a career bureaucrat of epic obliviosity.

---

[52] One way or the other, just about all government agencies are regulatory agencies.

Tony chuckled and said, "Well, working for Boss is like this—we are on the same flight down from Washington. I go directly to my seat in coach. His seat is in coach, too, but he just takes the first empty seat in first class. The man holding the seat reservation arrives and politely points out that it's his reserved seat, but Boss refuses to move. 'I got here first, so the seat is mine,' he says."

At this exact moment, Boss himself appeared and joined the little group of five friends.

All but Tony gasped. Not pausing for a moment, Tony plunged ahead—

"The stewardess asks him to please move back to the coach seat, but he refuses. Then the head stew tries to coax him, but he still refuses to move. The first-class passenger is becoming upset. Tempers are fraying. The door is closed, the plane has pulled away from the gate, and he's the only reason the plane can't taxi out to take off. The head stew is at wits' end, so she calls the cockpit. The copilot, a very professional lady, emerges from the cockpit. She kneels beside him and whispers into his ear. Shock spreads over his face and he quietly moves to his seat in the coach section. Problem solved!

'Gee! Thank you! What did you say to him?' the head stew asks the copilot.

'I told him that the coach section is going to Atlanta but the first-class section is going only to Miami,' says the copilot."

All six guys laughed, and Boss laughed the hardest, never suspecting that he was the joke.

Lesson 11.1: All is lost if you don't hit the punchline.

Tony cleverly got to the punchline unscathed. He was a poised raconteur and far better than most at shifting gears on the fly.

In most situations like this, the storyteller would stop in midsentence upon Boss' arrival and then lamely attempt to change the topic by commenting on the weather. Embarrassment would be so obvious that even a Boss would have realized that he had missed something that was inappropriate, secret, or that he was the topic of discussion. Funny that would not have been.

There is no point to telling a joke unless you get to the punch line. In the vast majority of jokes, the punch line is the last line, but in the no-longer-private joke setting there are two bottom lines. The first bottom line is that you have to get to the punch line. The second bottom line is that the room will suddenly fall silent just a moment before you utter the punch line. So, what can the average Joe joke teller do to avoid aborting the no-longer private joke?

Tell short jokes to minimize the possibility of someone blundering into the group after your story is underway. Even if the latecomer is not a joke breaker like Boss, you lose if you stop to explain or worse still, start over. You can't tell a long joke well without audience participation, anyway. Brevity is the soul of wit.

Use jokes that place the indispensable vulgarity, descriptor, or key name early in the joke so it's not absolutely necessary later in the joke. It's possible to remodel some jokes. Tony deftly turned the copilot into a woman to get around a 'kneels down by him' ambiguity. It takes a quick study to pull off this kind of move on the fly, though.

Bowdlerizing the joke rarely works well.   You can rid most jokes of George Carlin's seven dirty words, but the cleansed joke almost always loses impact. Since most ears will figure out that you tried to clean things up to avoid sounding badly in front of the latecomer, you may succeed in insulting both the latecomer and the original listeners.   Then you'll be taken as a dirty-minded man who tells crappy jokes poorly and tries to cover his ass by pretending to be someone he isn't.

But what if the Boss tells a joke?

John's boss Bernie liked to open each of his staph meatings with a joke. If the truth be known, Bernie did not possess an exquisite sense of comedy. He did not allow that to hold him back, however.

At one staff meeting Bernie came in with a story, loudly claiming he'd just read it on DA's DoD classified wire:

"At 2 PM Eastern time today, President Reagan appeared before the entire US Congress, the Supreme Court, his Cabinet, and Nancy's Astrologer.

Reagan said he had good news and some bad news that on balance canceled out the good news.

The gallery clamored—it was a need for good news day, so they asked for the good news first.

So, Reagan says, 'The good news is that God has stepped up to the plate. The Angel Gabriel appeared in Jerusalem this morning to say that Jesus, Mohammed, Moses, and Buddha will all be resurrected at dawn tomorrow. They will immediately create an order for humankind to end all wars and to forever prevent ethnic conflicts. There will finally be peace on Earth and good will toward man.'"

Bernie smiled in a way that John had seen once before, at the El Raunchito. Then Bernie continued:

"The entire room erupted in pandemonium. Everybody had a problem. The Christian fundamentalists were on their knees praying, convinced that the world is ending. The liberals were wailing because minorities will be underrepresented. The hawks went bonkers because they were about to become unemployed. Had they not been wearing their Italian and Saville Row suits, the lawyers would have lined up at the windows, ready to leap.

Finally, order is restored. All present, with one voice, said, 'So what's the bad news?'

President Reagan said, 'Gabriel has reserved a block of rooms in Salt Lake City.'"

Bernie looked around the room. About a third of the troops were laughing, about a third of the audience was sitting quietly with a quizzical look on their faces, and once the others had politely chuckled, heads shook, and eyes rolled. Bernie's broad smile faded. Completely.

John got Bernie's joke, but could not muster up a fake laugh even though he knew it was going to cost him down the road with Bernie. John has to learn how to make the sounds and the appearance as if he is laughing.

Lesson 11.2: Laughing on demand is a marketable skill.

On the other hand, if as a manager your ego demands that everybody in the room laughs, do as they do on TV. That is, have the sergeant at arms toss out the boobirds and then hold up a LAUGH sign while playing a laugh track on the loudspeaker.

Wally and fun at work

Wally was prompted to think about taking a comfortable and well-funded early retirement when his widely admired VP manager retired. But the VP didn't really retire. He left ABC, Inc, and hired in at the ailing XYZ, Inc. A month later, the VP called to ask Wally to come take over the 42-staffer Technical Operations function at XYZ.

Feeling honored, Wally accepted the job offer, but when he stepped in the XYZ door, he found the situation far worse than the VP had known. Tech Ops was already dispirited and then things got worse; Wally's first assignment was to visit the European subsidiary and fire all eleven of the Tech Ops employees at that site, irrespective of their performances or contributions.

The XYZ situation was grim. Its premier product had lost patent coverage and sales were falling in every other sector, too. XYZ was alive but barely twitching. Teamwork had gone out the door. Every rat that knew how to swim had fled the sinking ship and life jackets were on back order at the company store. The XYZ Big Boys had already unloaded their stock because they saw the once-dreaded predatory lowball takeover as the best-case scenario.

The primary legacy of the previous Tech Ops manager was not a work accomplishment. It was the edict that every desk had to be cleared to naught but desk writing pad, desk lamp, and empty pen holder at the work's end each day. No pictures, no papers, chair squared up, desk lamp centered, waste basket emptied, and no evidence of work ever being done. Two of three managers had just fled with several more staffers to form their own contract consulting company. The word on the street was that XYZ was a risky place to work and that with the recent firings and staff exits, Tech Ops had sunk to the rank of being the company's leper colony.

A week after returning from the European Tech Ops ethnic cleansing, Wally requested use of the big conference room for a general Tech Ops staff meeting. Because no higher-ranking department wanted it on February 2, Wally was allowed use of the big room.

Reflecting on the date, Wally somehow found a ballerina's tutu and wore it over his suit at the 2/2 staff meeting. The meeting had a serious, complete agenda. Wally ensured that the entire list of agenda topics was covered in a responsible manner. Appropriate records were kept, assignments made, and good jobs properly credited.

But somehow, in the presence of the hilarity generated by this distinguished-looking, silver-haired man with careful diction and polished manner conducting the meeting while wearing a pink tutu, Wally was able to keep a straight face.

Lesson 11.3: It's OKAY to be a little silly sometimes

Wally's next triumph came in the spring. XYZ had a summer hours policy — by working an extra hour on Monday through Thursday, the employees were to get Friday afternoons off. Since XYZ stock options were worthless and raises nonexistent, it was just about the only morale booster XYZ could afford to offer.

However, the previous manager insisted that **HE had to work** until late in the afternoon every Friday. When several senior employees decided the politically correct thing to do was to stay at work on Fridays until after the boss left, almost all of the employees felt obligated to work all afternoon on Friday. The summer hours perk thus turned into a morale destroyer; the troops saw it as the boss' and company's ploy to get 44 hours of work for 40 hours of pay.

When the first Friday in June rolled around, Wally wished everybody he met a pleasant weekend as he left the office building at the stroke of noon. The staff caught his message that very day and followed him out the door. That whole summer, Wally recalled, the offices were completely vacant on Friday afternoons when he came back to work at 1:15 to clean up his week's unfinished tasks.

In a year, Wally moved Tech Ops from being a bad workplace to a good workplace. A year later, when profitability at XYZ improved as a result of new products hitting the market (with thanks in no small part to hard work by Tech Ops), instead of bottom fishing for culls and cast-offs, Tech Ops had first choice candidates applying and accepting jobs at competitive but not elevated salaries.

Remark: Wally was not at all afraid of looking a little silly when silly was needed. Showing the troops that he was taking advantage of the XYZ Friday afternoon perk was inspired. He had a ready smile, but he didn't compile all those accomplishments by charm and wit alone; his staff did their jobs well, and were happy while doing it. Wally was a master of making himself the fall guy for his own jokes but somehow not letting the audience lose sight of the organizational goals.

What makes funning work?

Preparing the seed bed helps. Your audience needs to know when it's okay to have fun and laugh. New junior staff are pretty cautious about senior staff tongue-in-cheek stuff, so having a widely respected senior person act as a laugh shill helps.

Bernie's Mormon joke didn't fly. John thought it was intended to be semi-self-deprecating but not all took it that way. As jokes go, it was not that bad, but it was too long and his delivery only so-so. Pretending to read off a sheet of paper purported to be a printout from the DoD line would have helped. Again, having a manager as laugh shill would have helped a lot — a Master of Ceremonies could do this for you.

The management terms examination ploy worked but some found it offensive. Non-sequitur jokes work, but we find them surprisingly hard to integrate into the meeting flow. Puns work better than you'd think they might; they are rarely really funny but precipitating a massive audience groan is probably as therapeutic as a good laugh. The big advantages to puns are that they are easy to set up and can be made to appear to spontaneously spring from the text of the discussion. And, on average, puns tend to be less offensive than run-of-the-mill jokes.

Successful communication is everything in humor. As Henri showed, we always need to work on broadening our communication skills and perspectives. All cultures have wisdom to offer and the wise observer carefully weighs each particular granule of wisdom before dismissing it.

Books on public speaking steer the novice away from mixing humor with serious matters. Um, maybe a little too prudent. While it's hard to take your serious topic too seriously, it's way too easy to take yourself too seriously. If you give your totally serious talk in a totally serious manner, you're not allowing the listeners to catch their breath. But then, when they do catch their breath, they'll have lots of laughs about what a self-important ass you've become.

You can't make bread without a pinch of salt, and you shouldn't try to give a powerful talk on a serious matter without giving the audience a pinch of relief.

A little humor goes a long way. Understated is way better than overstated. A little bit of high-quality humor amid straight stuff will be memorable, but as in situation comedies, drollery gets blurred by excess so-so mirth.

A small measure of silly is an excellent antidote for the stuffed shirt image of management. But silly spreads like an oil slick so it must be measured with an eyedropper. Serious issues are serious issues. Management and staff cannot afford to lose sight of what needs to be accomplished.

What doesn't work?

Self-deprecating humor goes over better than boastful humor, but humorously deprecating others is way worse than over-the-top boasting. Racist, sexist, and otherist humor brings down the house in some circles but brings out the hook in others.

In the end, humor has to be tailored for the audience. As the anvil salesman[53] told Professor Harold Hill, you have to know the territory.

We once tried to work the expression "shot ourselves in the foot" for a few laughs. The slide showing crosshairs centered on large bare foot went over like a lead balloon. The Orientals in the room found the picture of the bare foot extremely offensive. Cross-culture humor is treacherous.

---

[53] The anvil salesman was Charlie Cowell. He knew the territory, had Hill figured out, became Hill's archenemy, and exposed Hill as a fraud, but Hill won anyway.

There are no universal jokes. But does this mean a manager should not attempt to bring good humor to the workplace? No. Sincere laughter in the workplace can be a manager's most powerful tool to lighten the mood on a grim day, to ease group tensions, to defuse conflicts, or to promote cooperation. Humor can drive a point home. Humor works way better than force to turn a lackadaisical workplace into a focused setting.

Almost everything can be accomplished with humor. But almost everything includes the good, bad, and indifferent. Yes, some won't get any joke, any joke will annoy some people, and any joke can cause a few to claim to be grievously offended, but the payoff among those who do laugh and enjoy the funning is simply too great to ignore.

Chapter 12

Caught up in Catch Phrases

In the '90s, the management gurus preached that we **must** "Walk the walk to talk the talk". All who held any hope whatsoever of being successful managers had to walk the walk before talking the talk, they averred. It **had** to be.

Our reaction then was, "Oh, piffle!" As obviosities go, the slogan itself was okay, but if anybody was talking without walking, it was a '90s management guru!

It's now twenty-some years later, and we're still torn between the enlightenment of cynicism and the burden of compulsion. We're sure that "Walk the walk to talk the talk" was just a catch phrase. But we do agree that walking should count for more than talking, so our conscience prevents us from blithely tossing this lightweights' slogan aside. Maybe we can learn something useful if we follow up on this. Let's find out.

Contributing, bragging, and succeeding

For starters, we're switching to terminology that tells it like it is. We're replacing "walk" by "contribute" and "talk" by "brag".

Do managers find success by maximizing contributing and minimizing bragging? Umm—not so you'd notice. It depends on how you define "success", though. There are lots of productive managers who tend to rely on letting their work speak on their behalf. However, in our 40-some years of observation, the loudest voices we've heard came from corner offices. The subdued types tended to toil away at managing, coaching, and hands-on work at their desks in the cubicles.

What about the extreme case? Are there successful managers who have zero bragging games and get ahead solely on the merits of their contribution games? Yes, there probably are some. But this is like speculating on the existence of life in other galaxies—surely somewhere there must be a dude in a remote cube farm, doing his arcane tasks, never blowing his own horn, and yet somehow pre-posthumously collecting his due for work well done.

So, could you get away with just contributing and letting your good work do all the bragging? Ah—we doubt it. In the current milieu, trash talk is so rampant that those who let their work do all their self-promoting get left behind.

Now, let's consider the braggarts in the workplace. On average, they do well company ladder-wise, but how do their contributing games stack up? In the extreme case, are there managers who claim great games but make no discernible contributions—and there's not a soul around who can remember when these big boasters were contributing? Good grief, the woods are full of 'em. Who hasn't worked for a guy like that?

The bottom line

So, is it that you can't get along with just contributing, but can you get ahead with just self-promotion? Maybe not right at first. But if it ever comes down to choosing between naught but contributing versus naught but boasting, opt for boasting. The odds of climbing over others on the company ladder are way better for the boasters than for the guys who don't pound their own drum. As we can infer from the news from Washington, DC, quietly doing your job is like paying taxes; it's for chumps.

Lesson 12.1: Blowing tunes on your own horn has become the skill of the realm. Sadly, in today's world, boasts, not deeds, are the *sine qua non*.

Case Study

At this point, it's time to move on to a case study. All we can offer, though, are some ideas. We know of no direct repudiations of the "Walk the walk to talk the talk" proverb. This is because every "successful" manager we've ever known claimed that he'd busted his butt back in the day. Even the shallowest salesman will bloviate on how he must bleed sweat to lubricate his glib tongue.

How can the Big Boys brag without contributing?

The Big Boys' magic words allow them to make claims that sound great but are so damn slippery that the claims can't quite be disproven. For this, fog shovelers are kept on retainer, and these fog shovelers do the heavy lifting—in fact, the "Walk the walk to talk the talk" catch phrase came from a fog shoveler's pen. These fog shovelers read the trade journals and mine out the latest phraseology. They are in-depth networked. They have huge expense accounts and hire gag writers just like Jay Leno does—the difference is that the fog shovelers' guys work on gag reflexes while Leno's guys work on gag jokes.

With the fog shovelers doing the writing, the Big Boys are freed up to put their best efforts into talking. Time-worn but successful concepts and procedures are clothed in bright, fresh new words. Since these concepts and procedures are mostly just paraphrases of what the Big Boys are already doing, the new words conveying the old ideas are a glorious reaffirmation that the Big Boys have been making all the right decisions all along.

Make no mistake; though, there is fearsome power in words that say what ears are eager to hear. Once, as legend holds, slick new words for old ideas smote a DA Board Director into utter enthrallment. With his 87-year-old brain clouded and being only semi-continent, he lost control while dashing to the loo. He slipped in the puddle of pee, fell, broke his hip, and died from post-surgery pneumonia. A tragedy, to be sure, but an eloquent testimonial to the level of inspiration attained that day by DA's management's words.

But Big Boys can't get along on just slogans and gags and words; they need to be steered, too. So, the fog shovelers' other key service is providing the Big Boys with an ear to the ground. Groundswells are usually fact-driven, though, and since these days even alternative facts can be checked, fog shovelers carefully heed these groundswells and guide the Big Boys away from checkable topics. It wouldn't do to have the

Movers' and Shakers' exquisite phraseology subjected to a Philistine's harsh light of truth.

How can you join the ranks of the successful boasters?

This brings us to the central issue of this chapter. We're at odds with the gurus' decrees that to be successful, managers can't brag without contributing. We know of too many exceptions.

Can you, Joe Competency, climb the company ladder by working around this walk-the-walk directive? Maybe. The Wonder Boys get away with it, but they have access to riches and resources. How can you emulate the Wonder Boys on a beer budget?

It's such a pleasant dream. If you could make old but sound ideas seem new and clever by just using new terms, as the Big Boys do, just think of the possibilities!

Imagine the smog in the room! If you can barely see the far end of the conference table when you rise to speak, just think of how much harder it will be for the plebian back-row bean counters and fact checkers who can't so much as score seats at the table. They won't contradict your graphics because they won't be able to read them. Only your shill or someone naively willing to display his ignorance will dare to ask you to explain. And then, if you have planted or cleverly anticipated the question, your glossy explanation will leave the room gasping at how thick the questioner has become in his old age. You'll be home a hero, with oak leaf cluster!

The task ahead

It's time to get back to reality. How can you become a bragger without having to do all that messy contributing stuff? If you are an ordinary competent guy, you can't. You can't begin a real manager's job on Planet Earth by stepping through the door as a star and blowing your own horn in the board room. Real managers' jobs begin in prosaic circumstance; you have a job, and you need to do it. To do your job, you'll need a contributing game and a self-promoting game.

Getting your contributing game in order is easiest, so do that first. You just have to turn on your brain, and flip your dumbass-move, bad-plan, no-no-no, and good-god-no! response toggles to the "off" positions. Then read your job description, do what it says to do, make sure your troops do the same, and keep up to date with the technology. And check in with the boss every now and again for input on what and how. Others might call that sucking up but we know better.

Now we're ready to work on self-promotion. Herein lies the action. Compared to contributing, the technologically oriented manager will find bragging harder to master. This is because most techie guys aren't that glib to begin with and they hardly ever get remedial training in fog shoveling.

The bragging game is way harder for the techie guy to maintain, too, because terminology is everything in the bragging game and terminology evolves at the speed of sound. The forces driving new terminology cause it to veer away tangentially from existing language. In contrast, technology evolves and then dissolves into obsolescence because new technology is typically built to extend and enhance existing technology.

To be out in front in terminology, you need to be into brand new terms or novel recycling of old terms in fresh and unexpected ways. It's a lot like jokes—new jokes are funnier than old jokes because regardless of how funny the old jokes might have been, it takes a skillful wag to get big laughs out of recycled punch lines.

The quest for words

But how do you get the words? You can't use last year's words. However accurate and appropriate they may have been, they just won't perform to your advantage this year. The "new reality" is the old reality. "Leveraging resources" is so pre-10s. "Pre-10s" is totally passé. Passé is hopelessly passé. "Cutting edge" has long since been dulled by use. The "foreskin of science" fell into the bris abyss a lifetime ago. "Sharpening your saw" went out soon after "buggy whips", and they fell out of style—jeez, did they even have calendars back then? Didn't they keep track of time by cutting notches on sticks? You gotta have new words and brand-new spins on old words

New words and spinning old words

There are two options for getting new words and making old words spin your way:

Poaching

The first way is **direct poaching**. But don't be satisfied with poaching off basic fog shovelers; focus on the deep-thinking fog synthesizers. Stay abreast with the best by poaching off the best.

Poaching gets off to a bad start though, because the Big Boys pay a lot for their fog shovelers' input and hot new terms aren't to be squandered at meetings attended by the hoi polloi. It just won't do to allow these wondrous new words to be on the street only minutes after they are uttered.

The best new terms will be unveiled at closed door sessions where the bucks have the most zeroes and the rollers are highest. Only the anointed and their management training toadies will hear. The venue doors will be locked tight and nigh impossible to penetrate. You might get in if disguised as a waiter or visual aids assistant, but you'll be toast when security figures out that you are pirating the flashy new words for your stale ideas. A disguise might get you in once, but you'll need continuity and at best you'll get the one trip to the well.

An emerging alternative poaching strategy is to **retain a hacker**. The top rank fog shovelers will likely do their thinking and prepping on computers. If there are words on a computer somewhere, these words can be accessed by another computer somewhere else. There are lots of guys out there who hack for hire, but they just take the price tag for an ultra-high-end training program at a posh retreat and tack on the nefarious activity surcharge.

So, with a limited budget, most likely you're going to have to wait for the word gurus' second wave of presentations at high, but not ultra-high, training programs. Access to this level of programs is easy; the only disguise you'll need to get in the door is a thick wallet.

Resurrect old terminology

Recycling is the second general approach to mastering fog shoveling. This is less costly and much less likely to lead to confrontation with a meeting sergeant-at-bouncing, but it's lots more work. It involves reading and thinking and learning terminology. You will have two advantages, though:

- The first thing that's broken your way is that there is a tremendous amount of discarded and obsolete terminology out there. It's in libraries, superseded management books, and on the internet. Much can be accessed by electronic dumpster diving.

- Your second leg up is that the typical new terminology maven is always cleansing his hard drive to make room[54] for the new stuff. Hence, his memory for old stuff will be patchy at best. Yes, he'll likely recall his wife's name, his pornfile password, and maybe his kids' names, but when he gets into the serious stuff — well. We know better.

The maven's insatiable appetite for new terminology drives unrelenting pressures that squeeze old words into his archives. Once archived, the old words are not

---

[54] This kind of guy won't start his career with a lot of room on his hard drive, if you get our drift.

merely forgotten; they are disremembered. These guys live, breathe, and think about new words. Their long-range planning is what's for next week. They could not give a smaller care about last month's ideas. So, the supply of discarded management phraseology is endless. And, the opportunities for recycling management phraseology are wide and deep.

The Agonizing Reappraisal

All of the above sounds possible, but the direct-poach and resurrect-old-words methods of finding hot terminology are both fundamentally dumbass ideas. They require getting ahead of the in-crowd on the in-crowd's turf. You might use language they actually understand. Can't have that. The bottom line is that you can't hang a consistent snow job on expert fog shovelers because you can't con a con man and you can't promote a promoter.

A new look at the problem

You want to burst onto the management scene as a messiah. You want to command the CEO's private conference room. You want to floor the CEO's Big Boys with your brand-new ideas and brilliant, clever plans.

But this is not easy. Even if you are super competent, brilliance is always in short supply and recognized brilliance is scarcer still. There's the ignorance issue, too; you can't burst into the CEO's conference room if they won't tell you which building the damn room is in. Then, if you do find the right building but get caught by the security guard, the son of a bitch will put your photo a company-wide Be-On-The-Lookout-For poster.

What can you do?

You could try being reasonable. You want to be a fog shoveler par excellence, but frontal assaults won't work. You aren't going to win by plunging headlong at the fog shovelers' greatest strength. You'll be way better off eluding the center of the fog shovelers' line and attacking their flank instead.

Ideas for workarounds

Again, we can call on our experience. We think you have two avenues:

The cross-discipline consultant

Turning yourself into a consultant might be within your reach and if so, is likely to be lucrative. Consultants rub elbows with the Big Boys so they often get early knowledge of, and input to, the listings for the really top-drawer job openings.

We know a lot about consultants; all successful consultants must come from far away. Their briefcases are worn to a fine patina, they grunt a lot, and they don't bother with deodorant. Appearances are not everything, but it helps to have gray hair and be a little tweedy looking. If there is a moustache, it must be unstained — only a pure white and bushy cookie duster will do. Bow ties used to be *de rigueur* but are now condemned as affectations.

What's hard is to accumulate the very substantial expertise needed to become a legitimate consultant, so a side door is needed. We think your best bet is to be the cross-discipline consultant. These guys have expertise that is related to, **but not central to**, the topic calling for their advice.

A good example of this phenomenon is the guy whose primary credential for the VP of Marketing job is that he was once a running back at Clemson. Yes, indeed, the guy who can claim to be an expert in one field has a leg up in almost any other field.

The cross-discipline consultant can demand premium compensation for knowing things that others don't know and speaking in terms that the audience finds unfamiliar (i.e., new) and yet comforting (i.e., sweet sounding terms that resist clear understanding). The cross-discipline consultant uses his slip-stream language to deflect questions of principal, process, and practicality, and then turns these pitfalls into benign questions of clarification.

You'll need to define and groom your expertise billing as an avocation in an obscure or out-of-reach field. Your choice of expertise options is essentially unlimited and up to your personal preferences. We can only offer a few wants and don't wants:

You'll want an avocation with a rich lexicon of insider terminology. The avocation needs to sound sexy and must have few cognoscenti — so few that you will know all their names and how to arrange to be absent from forums where they are present. You'll need lots of brand-new, pithy, actiony-sounding aphorisms, too. "The dog don't hunt" works elsewhere, but won't cut it in this context.

You'll not want any field of serious science as an avocation. Learning the science would be hard to do and keeping current in the field even harder. But most importantly, you are trying to wow the 99% talk/1% substance types, and they have long since dismissed every field of science as a bother.

The avocation should be a bit veiled. Collecting would be pitiful and doing anything with models would be almost as bad, except for maybe the high fashion types and that approach is too expensive for the working guy. No hope for anything in music, either, because music is too important for way too many people. Golf could be sexy enough if your scores are close to scratch, but it's far too common and as sure as we'll meet damnation one day there will be someone who insists on playing you. Same thing with fine wine. Gourmet coffees, perhaps, but only in a far-side backwater setting.

Sailing is sexy enough and has lots of good nautical terms, but too many will know about sailing and many will have some familiarity with the terms. Sailing around the world is mucho sexy, but there is too much press coverage — anyone who is interested will be able to find out if you actually showed up in Pago Pago. Besides, Samoa is overrun with college football recruiters who hold lines of communication to bookies everywhere. Bora Bora is not as risky, but remember, you **can not** afford to get exposed as a fake.

Ice boating is rugged and sexy, but the lexicon is like conventional sailing, so it's understood too well. Piloting an ultra-light might be okay, but the usual light plane is way too common and the private plane Mile-High Club is a one-trick pony.

Bungee jumping and zip lining are hopelessly egalitarian. Hang gliding is better. Probably the coolest would be these webs-between-the-legs-and-arms suits they use to dive off mountains.

Spelunking would be good—very few bored room guys will ever go crawling through caves, the caving lexicon is rich with creepy terms, the crawling creatures can be imagined as innumerable and lethal, and with so many real hazards there are tons of foreboding circumstances.

Asking the penetrating question

The second avenue to CEO country requires years of preparation. It's learning how to ask penetrating questions. These are questions that lead the audience to see new possibilities, to understand different perspectives, and to consider new approaches and points of view. If you can lead the audience into believing that your questions were the catalysts that drew their brilliant ideas into focus, they will think they are way smart. If that happens, you'll put yourself way out ahead of the peloton[55] of wannabes.

But formulating the clever, insight-inducing question is very hard. Most young managers are a whole lot better at answering questions than asking questions because our educational systems are based on learning answers to questions.

A student is deemed to be good when he answers many questions aimed at exposing weaknesses in his knowledge base. Excellent students go a step beyond; they figure out how to build on their knowledge bases to answer

---

[55] The mob of also-runners who are bunched up behind the leaders in a bicycle race is a peloton.

questions that require in-depth understanding of the subject matter. The top stage in these excellent students' growth is learning out how to pose these in-depth questions.

Many techies are willing to invest the careful thought and hard work needed to pose penetrating questions in their subject area. What sets the experts apart from the also-rans is finding the words that so succinctly state their questions that even the Big Boys understand the questions, the questions' imports, and the implications.

When you do get to speak in CEO country

Okay, let's suppose that you have been invited to speak before the Big Boys. You have done your homework and think that one or more of the Big Boys **is on your side**. You have your brain primed with several very clever insight-inducing questions that will surely plant the seeds for your ideas. You have your shit together. You expect to clarify thinking, change balky minds, and have a significant impact on what the company is going to think and do during the next year.

But what's really going to happen? If you don't have an out-of-this-world-clever plan or a powerful advocate seated at the right hand of the CEO, the cadre of Big Boys' gun-bearers and other courtiers are going to have you for lunch.

Why is this? Like the fog shovelers, the Big Boys' courtiers have two roles. The first is to offer knowledgeable advice on matters of detail, suitable weaponry for problem resolution, and clever words to dress up issues of concern. These groupies' second role is to prevent the Big Boys from even hearing, and certainly from accepting, new ideas put forth by anyone except one of their own sanctioned Big Boy staff. These courtiers have their turf, and they are going to defend it. For this reason, the new ideas you want to implant must seem to spring from the minds of the Big Boys.

There is another closely related issue. This approach, i.e., leading the Big Boys into actual understanding of what is being discussed, is diametrically opposed to the old baffle-them-with-bullshit tactic. This should be a totally good thing, except the Big Boys will be up to their asses with advisers and boasting game toadies who routinely utilize the baffler ploy. Since it's the advisers' missions to discredit new outside thought, the baffler ploy will be the first thing the courtiers think of when you utter your first three syllable word.

It takes a keen command of the language to convince those who don't want to be convinced.   You'll need persistence, too, and unless you make a good first impression, you won't get a chance to practice your persistence.

So, good luck with your pitches and presentations. Study earlier presentations and do your homework. Make your graphics premium vanilla and make friends in high places. Read the body language in the audience and listen carefully to the other speakers. Embrace the emerging new terms in your field and introduce a few new terms from other fields but only when the terms appear to fit well.

But put your best efforts into formulating penetrating questions to ask the chair, the other speakers, and the audience.

Mornings are better than afternoons. Evening sessions are mixed bag because of the cocktail hour. Get the opening or closing speaker slot. If you are good, you'll be noticed and possibly groomed as a protégé. If you are bad, you'll be noticed and possibly groomed as a diamond-in-the-rough reclamation project. If you are so-so, you'll be forgotten. So be either good or bad.

And, whatever you do, don't run over your allotted time.

Lesson 12.2: Brevity is the greatest of all self-rewarding virtues.

Chapter 13

Exceptional Personnel Selection

This chapter is directed toward selecting staff for difficult, unusual techie jobs that don't pay well and involve strenuous, ambiguous work environments, but require a high level of motivation. Gee. This sounds like military service. Maybe we can piggyback on military recruiting?

The Marine recruiting system

Isn't it a marvel how the Marines can recruit all the guys they need in spite of their legendarily hard-ass drill sergeants in addition to their super hazardous duty assignments? They get first pick from thousands of guys who don't mind the low pay and are just aching to get browbeaten and then get a shot at getting shot. The inescapable conclusion is that the Marine recruiting strategy is top notch. Since their recruiting works so well, do you suppose using the Marine approach would help us find just the right techie for a tough assignment? Let's check this out.

The Marines look for the smart and ultra-tough. They start by luring in a "few good men" with their "Marine Look" posters featuring studs brimming with testosterone, wearing impeccable dress blues, and sporting classic high-and-tight jarhead hairdos. The Marines find these guys who "look like Marines" and somehow this appearance-driven recruiting homes right in on precisely the warriors needed for our upcoming amphibious invasion of Bazookastan or guarding our embassy in Outer Noreturnia.

Let's see how the Marine strategy fits into techie recruiting. The Marines want a few good men. We want a few good techies. So far, so good. Marines and techies have to be smart and resourceful. Check. Marines and techies have to perform intelligently under pressure. Check. Marines and techies must quickly learn and then utilize new technologies. Check.

Comparing Marine and techie tasks doesn't go so well, though. These days, what with all the bad publicity and mergers, the few techie companies still performing offshore mercenary tasks sublet all their wet work. Further, techie security work is only remote-site surveillance with videocams and sensors. At best, an itty-bitty check.

Marines always look and act like Marines, but techies might be any of the SLBGQQTNA[56] persuasions, sloppy dressers, have long hair, and they come in all sizes, shapes, and colors. Searching by experience credentials fails, too, because the inexperienced but fresh mind is often the techie's greatest asset. Techies are like steins of beer; regardless of how fancy the stein might be, it's still the beer that matters. No check at all.

Okay, appearances haven't helped, so let's think about following orders. Marines must understand and precisely obey orders. Techies must understand which orders to obey, to ignore, and to frankly disobey. Sheesh! We'd need an anti-check to score this attribute.

---

[56] SLBGQQTNA: Straight, Lesbian, Bisexual, Gay, Questioning, Queer, Transsexual, Not Applicable

The Marines' system works for them but not for us

Too bad. The Marine strategy is of no help at all for selecting techies. Our hope for a shortcut to finding good personnel has taken us nowhere. We are left with what we knew when we started — that the worst employees are those who either do nothing their managers tell them to do or do precisely what their managers tell them to do. We still need to use our brains as we hire, assign rewards, and promote.

It's time to roll up the sleeves and get on with selecting personnel for specific tough tasks. It's Case Study time.

Case Study

Background for a Desert Aromatics Case Study

For years, John's BS&P bunch at DA had toiled into nights and holidays to get the data input function of their site-specific Orr-Allee Data Entry and Database Management System into fully operational status. Then, one glorious Thursday morning in late May, 1998, John told Bernie that the moment had come to slay the fatted calf. All the testing data from Bernie's entire empire were in the Orr-Allee data base. All could rejoice, for Bernie's realm was completely d-based.

On that festive Thursday, all in BS&P went home happy. For most, it took a long time to get home. On Friday, many called in sick, needing to rest, repent, soothe vocal cords, and heal hangovers. Monday was Memorial Day. The DA Annual Stockholders' Meeting convened Tuesday morning.

The politics of the situation

Were there mint juleps in shaded hammocks for BS&P on Tuesday? Um, not quite. While the BS&P workers sweated out the acetaldehyde on Friday, Orr-Allee's blood enemy competitor Aine announced two things:

1. A terrific new competing product.
2. Aine had lured Turner Allee away from Orr-Alee and this new product was branded Aine-Allee. Orr-Alee was only an input system, but Aine-Alee was an output system that digested data and managed everything else, too. Aine-Allee was superior[57] to Orr-Allee in every regard.

On Monday evening, the DA Big Boys had been swept away in a tsunami of Aine-Allee infatuation at a vendor-sponsored, by-invitation-only, premium-booze cocktail party. About 2:00 AM on Tuesday morning, drunk as lords and unduly eager to show the DoD brass that DA was a cutting-edge operation after all, the DA Big Boys "scored a **STEAL**" as a full-fee Gamma Test Site for Aine-Allee.

To further enhance the disaster, as the Big Boys wallowed in Aine-Alee's promises of stupendous output, they fell head over heels in love with the sales rep, Ms. Aine-Allee. She looked and walked like Kim Kartrashian does today. In stark contrast, poor Ms. Orr-Alee was a fine, competent, and well-groomed lady, who looked and walked like Ms. No Nonsense Panty Hose.

After informing no one but the CEO's KNAFE (Knows Not Ass From Elbow) hangers-on and certainly neither John

---

[57] "Superior", and "breathtakingly costlier" are precisely synonymous terms.

nor his BS&P staff, Bernie announced at the Tuesday morning opening of the Stockholders' Meeting that DA would adopt Aine-Allee "with all due haste". This created a stir, but an even bigger stir came at noon, when Ms. Aine-Allee was cornered and forced to confess that the production version of Aine-Allee would not be available for installation for 18 months.

In corporate America, the only way the Big Boys will tolerate the risk of a systems upgrade damaging earnings is if they can cower behind a kudos-worthy news item for the annual report and meeting. So, after intense and blood-spilling Boared Rheum negotiation, "with all due haste" was defined as 24 months. The Aine-Allee implementation news would be postponed until the 2000 Annual Meeting.

Bernie came from the Boared Rheum boasting that he'd gotten John 24 months to get Aine-Allee in place. What John actually got was 18 months to screw around with half-baked Aine-Allee prototypes and 6 months to bring the production version of Aine-Allee online and integrated with the ongoing work being done on DA's site-specific version of Orr-Allee. The hooker was the assumption that Aine-Allee would actually be delivered in 18 months. John was sure there'd be no way from hell he'd see even a stable version of Aine-Alee in 18 months, let alone a production version.

What John is facing

It was tacit that the DA Big Boys' enthusiasm for Aine-Allee was fueled by enhancements in alcohol input rather than by enhancements in work output. The other elephant sharing John's bathtub was that Turner Allee had been the guru-level deity who had managed every aspect of Orr-Allee product support. Now, with Allee gone, Orr-Allee product support was in limbo. All that was left behind were Orr-Allee product manuals. They precisely met industry standards, i.e., understood only by those who already understood everything about the system. For novices, the Orr-Allee manuals were distractions at best, giving a little less than no help at all.

But regardless of product support, DA management demanded that John's organization maintain full production status with Orr-Allee throughout the transition to Aine-Allee. In view of headcount freezes and usual staff turnover, at best John had a slim chance of maintaining DA's Orr-Allee staffing at a skeleton crew level until Aine-Allee came online. Further, he had not a single staffer who knew more than rumored pre-release folklore about what Aine-Allee was supposed to do, let alone was trained on it.

John's specs for the transition-driving employee

John's plan was to identify a very capable lead[58] worker, obtain training for the worker, and have the worker steer the BS&P efforts to harmonize Aine-Allee with Orr-Allee. The worker would be called the Senior Aine-Allee Systems Specialist (the SAASS). Beyond the inevitable staffing deficit, finding this worker was a daunting challenge because:

a) In-depth expertise in both Orr-Allee and Aine-Allee systems was required.

b) DA BS&P expertise was needed to exploit system and process synergisms.

---

[58] That's lead as the guy up in front, not lead as in the guy down in back.

c) High level communication and teaching skills were required for training.

d) Writing skill was needed for integrated operational documentation and SOPs that were actually understood and followed.

The SAASS was to learn how to operate the prototypes of Aine-Allee a full year before the stable version of Aine-Allee came online. The SAASS would then help choose and train an associate. Together, the SAASS and associate would master the DA Orr-Allee/Aine-Allee interface, resolve conflicts, and exploit the deluge of benefits Ms. Aine-Allee claimed would surely rain down following conversion from Orr-Allee to Aine-Allee.

Unfortunately, the Orr-Allee staffing history was an eagle-sized fly in John's ointment. Orr-Alee had always been staffed by non-managers, so according to Bernie, John was boxed into making the SAASS a tech leader holding no management authority. The SAASS job would be technically difficult, carry low authority but high accountability, and bear a crappy salary.

Remark: John has done okay in determining personnel needs and restrictions. Now, does he recruit outside or repurpose someone from among the current employees?

Hint: John was inclined to give insiders a chance but Bernie thought most of the department staff were dopes.

Management obstacles

Since John needed a job opening before hiring from the outside and the company-wide headcount was frozen, he figured he'd have to use his body with Della to just get her to add his request for an opening to Bernie's waiting list. And then, to actually obtain the opening, he'd have to surrender a long-term lease on his soul to Bernie and the Big Boys. John doubted, too, that he could find an outsider who was even close to ready to step into the SAASS job.

Bernie strongly favored going outside to find "a guy who looks like a Marine—a leader" to fill the job. Not surprisingly, Bernie prevailed. He ordered John to contact HH, Bernie's fav headhunter. When John protested that he had no opening, Bernie promised that if John used only HH, a headcount variance could be had.

John knuckled under and called HH. HH was known to be KNAFE in spades for both Orr-Allee and Aine-Allee, but this didn't worry HH. "Not a problem at all," he contended. "In fact, it's an advantage, because it frees me to consider all the options with recruiting."

John had no retort ready for this specific disclaimer, so he just held the line.

After a long pause punctuated by sounds of HH shuffling papers, HH spoke. "John! I've got your **perfect** guy! He solves differential equations in his sleep and then has wet dreams in hexadecimal! You're soooo in luck, buddy—you DA guys are such good customers that I'm giving you first chance on him—his resumé paper is still warm! You better take him now—if you wait until this afternoon, he'll be gone to Taytes!"

"But I'm trying to hire a guy to take us from Orr-Alee into Aine-Allee. I need a top gun in software," John protested.

HH shifted gears. "A computer guru, Johnny? No sweat. I've got your guy."

"But I don't want a hardware guy," John insisted, "it's a software problem."

"Johnny, baby," HH cooed, "if this guy was any softer, we'd have feed him Viagra so he could stand up. Haw, haw, haw."

John's official reason for dismissing HH's candidates was lack of knowledge about Aine-Alee and DA's Orr-Allee operations. The real reason was that HH was a patronizing prick whose jokes were even worse than Bernie's.

Lesson 13.1: Calling a headhunter is easy and allows the hirer to blame the headhunter when things go wrong.

Remark: And headhunters are always spendy. But Bernie bought into HH's hype that hiring a no-worries-mate-he's-already-trained guy was the only risk-free way to go. Either that, or maybe Bernie was getting a "referral incentive" from HH. This kind of thing happens, you know.

Bernie accepted John's refusal to hire one of HH's guys only because Bernie had come up with a better idea. He told John to go to Bernie's alma mater, a tech school where an Aine-Allee course had just been added to the catalog.

"This could be a fun trip for an unattached guy like you. Who knows? You might find a coed who really wants a job in an Aine-Allee shop," Bernie suggested, coyly adding, "and when you are ready to hire someone, there will be plenty of solid guys to choose from."

John called the tech school placement office instead. They had tons of resumés, but John could access only names, courses, and grade point averages. It was easy to ID those who got good grades. It was easy to understand, too, that since the Aine-Allee course was brand new, no student had completed it. The school had never offered training in Orr-Allee and claimed that they held no records of what their graduates did after graduation, so there were no records of grads with Orr-Allee training or experience, either.

John believed that hiring a tech school type without Orr-Allee experience or Aine-Alee training was a doomed, pig-in-a-poke operation. While pigs are indeed easily trained, they are still pigs, so John decided to forgo the recruiting trip to the tech school. He figured that the lack of Orr-Allee background would be an even bigger problem with the tech school job aspirants than with HH's offerings.

Bernie's outrage about stopping the tech school recruiting convinced John that cutting a deal with Bernie to gain an overrun headcount opening was a really, really bad idea.

After Bernie's vexation subsided, John proposed choosing an internal staff member who was already expert in DA's Orr-Allee. He'd then have the selected worker tutored by a trainer from Aine-Allee. In addition to the job being so poorly paid that no well-qualified outsider would consider it, John argued that an insider with DA Orr-Allee experience would be way better than an outsider at dissolving the blood clots in the Orr-Allee/Aine-Allee interface.

Bernie said "no" and he would have prevailed, but Ms. Aine-Allee had this Aine-Allee "expert" friend who lusted for bigger bucks and a cushy escape from work in the Aine-Alee hamster wheel. Ms. Aine-Allee told Bernie that he could buy expertise in both Orr-Allee and Aine-Allee if he hired her friend away from Aine-Allee.

But when Ms. Aine-Allee proudly told how precious her "expert" would be, Bernie went into apoplectic shock. "That's more than I make!" he screamed. The blow beneath Bernie's budget belt struck home. He was not about to jeopardize his annual bonus by running over budget.

Ms. Aine-Allee played hard ball and refused to enable an Aine-Allee trainer. This annoyed Bernie so much that he ignored the Big Boys' hots for Ms. Aine-Alee and their directive that the Aine-Allee contract was strictly hands-off. Bernie blew the whistle and cited an obscure training clause in the contract.

Fearing the training could be a deal and big commission breaker, Ms. Aine-Allee relented and provided a trainer.

John met with the trainer to learn Aine-Allee training needs and then moved to select a trainee from the Orr-Allee workers. HR wanted to run aptitude testing on selected staff. The staff clamored for self-nomination.

John resolved to prevent another party[59] from making the SAASS choice on his behalf, but his resolution went down the tube when conventional wisdom[60] installed Cy's senior Orr-Allee systems analysts Gunnar and Hugh and Mo's senior Orr-Allee techs Jane and Spiro on John's short list.

---

[59] Another party = the boss, union rules, seniority, or irrelevant credentials
[60] Conventional wisdom = Bernie's non-negotiables, as relayed to John by Della

Bernie directed John to choose among the four. "You got all the good ones," Bernie explained, "except for Spiro, they look like managers. The rest of that Mickey Mouse Orr-Allee bunch are nothing but riff-raff and losers."

Determined to put a name on the list that was not imposed by Bernie, John conducted a no-stones-left-unturned search among all the junior Orr-Allee users. Many sang praises of Maureen, a lowly data entry clerk who reported to the Grand Dragon of Data Entry, Gladys, VVA[61]. Gladys reported only to God but Gladys was below Cy on the org chart, so John cleared it with Cy before setting up an interview with Maureen.

Prior to the interviews, John asked each of the five interviewees to write an Orr-Allee data management routine, complete with explanations covering the routine's use, function, and applicability. The interviews began the following Monday.

Jane LaPlain

Tall and willow-like in her youth but now more ponderosa-like, **Jane's** appearance was nothing like a Marine's. She looked close to what you'd get if you asked an artist to draw "a caricature of a SAASS" — graying, bifocals, sensible shoes, hair in tight bun but with buns unrestrained, and face in perpetual scowl.[62] Her academic credentials were negligible and her training all on the job because she'd hired

---

[61] VVA—Vestal Virgins of America. Gladys claimed to be a charter member of the VVA. She had no wall plaque, but she was probably old enough.
[62] Oh, gee. This description sounds unkind. Let's put it this way—if Jane had been a plant instead of an animal, she'd have been wind pollinated.

into her spot in the earliest days of computerized data management.

Jane evaluated John as being just one more annoying book-smart young man who thought he knew much more than he really knew. So, she set out to dominate the interview. "I am the hardest worker in the department," she declared, "but it's not just my hard work and intelligence that sets me apart. In addition to my extraordinary gift of common sense, I have **experience**. I am the **ONLY** person who has worked on Orr-Allee since its introduction here at DA."

"The job is mine. Because of my experience, I am the SAASS. You wouldn't understand because you have been here only a year or two[63], but I know the **right** way to do things with Orr-Allee," she said. "And what's more, only I am qualified to train someone to replace me when I retire."

John cleared his throat as if to speak, but Jane stormed onward. "Since I am the only person in the organization with sufficient intelligence, work ethic, and experience to be the SAASS, just say I'm the SAASS and be done with it."

When John finally got a word in, he said he wanted to talk to the other candidates. Jane retorted that the interview was a waste of her valuable time, threw down her Orr-Allee routine writeup, and stomped out of the room.

Still believing that Jane's life was a constant flurry of high priority work performed at flank[64] speed, John spent the rest of the morning reviewing Jane's archives. It became clear why she was a key player on so very many ongoing projects—

---

[63] John had been in the department for about ten years at the time.
[64] Flank speed—A Navy expression meaning running at the ship's highest possible speed. The term probably arises from the concept of hauling ass at the max.

she worked on many but finished few. Her clientele comments file was even more telling; allowed, she might be a hell of a worker as everybody said, but agreed, when a crisis arose with an ultra-priority task, she always had a hyper-ultra-priority project that had to be finished first.

John surmised that Jane would always have an ultra-priority project on her desk because she only rarely finished her work on any project. And, there were more than a couple comments that she'd get more done if she didn't spend her time telling tales of DA's Orr-Allee early days. At this point, John went back to read Jane's performance reviews. Over the past five years the phraseology was essentially unchanged. John supposed Cy's admin was ghost writing new reviews by recycling old reviews.

Lesson 13.2: The manager's easiest way to ensure workers live up to their reputations is to recycle their old performance reviews.

John decided that Jane's amazingly weak productivity and her inability to complete tasks in a timely manner would seriously undermine her efforts as the SAASS. He was about to cross her off the list when he tried her Orr-Allee data management routine. It was nicely done and it worked so well that it changed his mind. John decided to keep her name on the Possible List.

Gunnar Rhea

Gunnar was one of the strongest systems guys in Bernie's fiefdom and surely top gun on DA Orr-Allee. Dressed in the classic Geek Revival Style, Gunnar looked like a SAASS, and when he spoke, he'd look at the floor but not right at his shoes. This indicated that as techies go, Gunnar was moderately extroverted and thus might have latent leadership potential.

Gunnar had once been accused of sexual harassment, but John allowed a pass on this; Gunnar spoke only in technospeak. In English, it was likely that Gunnar was so grammatically challenged that he couldn't tell a preposition from a proposition.

Gunnar's Orr-Allee routine and its writeup were so arcane that John couldn't get past step 1. When asked for clarification, Gunnar declared that those who failed to understand it were obsolete cretins.

Since effective communication was going to be a major part of the SAASS' function, John concluded that Gunnar would be a bad choice and crossed him off the list.

Hugh Briss

Hugh was a recent Bernie *wunderkinder* hire with limited Orr-Allee experience but two[65] Master's degrees from a high-end university. His were the highest paper qualifications of anyone working on Orr-Allee, and during the interview Hugh remarked that he had a stronger education from a better school than John.

Hugh was a basic I'm-right/you're-wrong kind of guy who looked and acted like the alpha male. John thought this could be an asset in a high-tech operation. John gathered that Bernie thought it would surely be a huge asset.

Hugh's take on the SAASS job was that with his special skills, the SAASS position would evolve into a full-blown senior management job in only a month or two. "I'll simply delegate the routine Aine-Allee operations and training tasks to 'an underling'. The organization cannot afford to use me in a less-than-optimal manner, so we'll just fit the job around me." Hugh closed by adding, "I find your Orr-Allee write-up request trivial and insulting."

Being sure that by no way in hell would Bernie allow the SAASS position to turn into a minor manager's slot, let alone a senior manager's slot, John concluded that Hugh's ego and ambition would be insurmountable barriers. And, with no Orr-Allee routine to support his candidacy, Hugh was dropped from the list of candidates.

---

[65] Since Master's degrees are often given as consolation prizes in PhD-heavy schools, two Master's degrees from the same school may indicate failure to complete not just one, but two PhD programs.

Spiro Keating

Spiro was an experienced Orr-Allee user who was so keen to be named the SAASS that he badmouthed Hugh and Gunnar during his interview.

According to Lawrence, in Bernie's opinion Spiro was too short and too greasy to promote. As a result, Spiro had never even been a temporary team leader, and this meant that career-wise, the SAASS job would be a step up for Spiro.

But Spiro wanted more than a step up. "I'll run the Aine-Allee show like it should be run. Give me a license, and I'll kick some asses for you!"

John surmised that Spiro would excel at kicking asses because he was such a perfect ass, but when John tried out Spiro's Orr-Allee routine it ran correctly on the first try. It then took John a minute to realize that the reason using Spiro's routine was so easy was that John had already used the routine. It was Jane's routine. John took another look at Jane's routine. Her entire routine package was a Xerox copy of Spiro's.

John concluded that Spiro was an ambitious jerk who wanted to be in charge. The woods are full of jerks who want to be in charge, but Spiro apparently knew his stuff and wrote well. He remained a possibility for the SAASS job.

Maureen Jones

John went into this interview holding little hope for **Maureen**. She had taken every allowed in-house training course and she had recently earned a night school associate degree, so she had more formal training than Jane. On the downside, she had a way weaker academic background than Gunnar, Hugh, and Spiro. What John found so discordant was that despite still being classified and paid as a never-promoted Step 1 data entry clerk, she was the DA Orr-Allee go-to for all the newbie techs and lots of the more experienced techs, too. Further, her fellow workers gave her kudos for teaching skills and making routines written by Gunnar and Hugh easier to understand.

Maureen was acutely intimidated by John and the interview. She'd just heard that Gladys was livid about John arranging the interview through Cy and expected that Gladys' payback to be hell. Being dressed in Wal-Mart couture didn't help Maureen's confidence, either.

After the tense beginning, though, Maureen's qualifications just seemed to get better. Until John looked at her Orr-Allee routine write-up. It was exactly like Spiro's! John was keenly disappointed and was barely able to keep his emotions in check.

"Maureen," he said, "I asked for **your** write-up and you gave me a copy of Spiro's. What's going on here?"

He did not say, "What IN HELL is going on here," but Maureen was terror stricken, anyway. "I don't know!" she protested. "I have no idea! I wrote the routine right after your invitation to interview arrived. I tested it and wrote the explanatory material. I've used it and let lots of others use it, too, and no one has had problems. My source initials are right there in the header comments. I thought it all checked out..." Her voice faded into a murmur as she slumped back in her chair, totally demoralized. Tears welled in her eyes but did not run down her cheeks.

John's first step after the interview was checking Spiro's routine. Uh-huh—the initials "MJ" were in the header.

John's findings and choice

After crossing off Spiro for blatant plagiarism and Jane for incompetent plagiarism, the only name left was Maureen. John knew Bernie would balk. The other managers and the senior Orr-Allee staff would resist, too, but John concluded that Maureen was the right person for the job for four reasons:

1. She started in data entry, the lowest rung of the Orr-Allee operation, and despite never being allowed a promotion, had worked above her grade and with every level of the Orr-Allee operation. She understood the nuts, bolts, and full spectrum of DA Orr-Allee data entry, data management, and data retrieval.

2. If an Orr-Allee tech needed help, Maureen was called. Every time. They didn't ask Hugh, Gunnar, or Spiro, and never Jane, because Jane was always too busy with work or anecdotes. Even Ms. Orr-Allee routinely requested that Maureen do the systems patch testing.

3. Maureen was a learner. She had taken and done well in every allowed training course. She learned Orr-Allee and could learn Aine-Allee, too.

4. She alone could be given a significant pay raise upon taking the job.

Maureen's downsides were her relatively few college level BS&P courses and at thirty years old, Gladys and others still dismissed her as a green untrained kid.

John's recommendation:

Satisfied that he had made his best effort to select the SAASS, John went to Bernie to get a buy-in. Bernie gave him a sell-out instead.

Things got ugly. Very ugly. "John! You pitiful pissant! I give you access to the best recruiter in town but you turn him down! I give you access to the best tech school in the nation, but you turn it down! You're handed a short list with the smartest, hardest working, most senior, best qualified, and most experienced workers in the organization and you choose a dumpy little clerk who has the worst credentials of the bunch. Tell me, John, is your pudgy potpie so good in bed that you are willing to lose your job for her?"

That afternoon, a calmer Bernie called John in to say that the best candidate, by far, had just visited his office. "She has outgrown her job and is ready to move on to something else. Instead of your clerk, I'm giving you Jenny, the best looking and smartest woman in the entire company. She has to get the job, because if she doesn't, she's out the door. I all but offered the SAASS job to her. Your ugly data clerk is unacceptable."

End of discussion. Bernie rose and sent John on his way. Della shooed John off her territory in the outer office, too.

The Agonizing Reappraisal

John set out to learn about Jenny. Lawrence said that Jenny was doing so-so as an engineer. Cy said that all the women and even some of the men working with her were disenchanted with her preening, prancing, and procrastinating. Everybody in the whole damn organization (except Bernie and Della, of course) agreed that Jenny's having never done a thing with Orr-Allee was more than sufficient to prevent her from being considered for the SAASS job.

John called Jenny for an interview anyway. Before he asked a single question, Jenny asked, "How can I be considered for the SAASS job when I have never worked with Orr-Allee?" She went on to say that the SAASS job might be interesting and challenging, but too much like hard work. Worse still, she saw that there was minimal chance for advancement and no fun potential at all.

And as for Bernie's concerns that she might walk if she didn't get the SAASS job? "Well, sure, I might. But I might walk if I get the SAASS job, too. I get offers all the time. Lots of old men want to hire me."

At that point, the interview ran off the tracks. "Maureen is a better choice for the SAASS job," Jenny said. "Maureen will do it better than I would, and she'll stay at it longer. I know, because we were in the same high school class—just acquaintances; not close friends. She was a little better student than I and prettier, but in a well-washed way. The other girls and the teachers liked her more, but I had way more friends among the boys. She was the valedictorian and I was the salutatorian. We were both in the Homecoming Queen court. But the one thing that set us apart, John, was that even though Maureen's dad was super strict, she got pregnant on Prom Night. My mom helped me with birth control. I just had a really fun time."

John saw need to talk with Maureen again. Maureen was visibly upset and did not respond to John's opening words, so John decided to wait her out. After what seemed like a week of silence, she asked in a trembling voice, "What did Jenny say?"

John said, "She thinks you're the better choice."

Maureen's face got all twisted up and her emotions took over. The dam holding back all the grim years burst. A half-box of Kleenex and two trips to the lady's room later, John had been told far more than he wanted to know about the Senior Prom pregnancy, the hasty marriage, and then the eight years of beatings. He learned about the cops pounding on the front door while her "snot-begotten breadloser[66]" husband fled out the back, her mother's stroke, her father's death, raising her daughters all by herself, and the years of night school. But most of all, he heard about the frustration of being the best but having a boss who refused to promote her because she was too good to lose.

John concluded that based on appearances, formal credentials, but mostly factoring in Bernie, Jenny was the clear winner. Based on the needs for the job and doing the job, Maureen was John's choice.

John took his recommendation to Bernie again.

Bernie went nuts again and called for Della, asking her to bring a pen and note pad. Calming himself, Bernie said, "Tell me again, John, why you are making this idiotic

---

66 John's, not Maureen's, terms of endearment

recommendation. Della, please write down what this fool says. I need his exact quote for the firing memo."

John repeated his recommendation and summarized his worksheets and notes. Apparently, something got lost, though, because the notification of John's termination never reached HR or John's inbox. Maureen was promoted to the SAASS position although Gladys and Della were really pissed about it and tried repeatedly to get Bernie to interfere.

Remarks: Three years post SAASS selection Qs and As.

Q. Was the production-quality edition of Aine-Allee delivered in 18 months?
A. Get real. It slid in under the door at 31 months, so the news was delayed until 2001.
Q. Did Maureen succeed in her training and documentation functions as the SAASS?
A. Yes.
Q. Did she master the SAASS position?
A. Depends on who you ask. The techs who work with Maureen and Aine-Allee users say YES! Maureen says she still has a lot to learn.
Q. Will Maureen continue to toil away as the SAASS for the foreseeable future?
A. Maybe. It comes down to whether the new Ms. Aine-Alee persuades Maureen to take the far, far better paid systems development job at the Aine-Alee systems headquarters in Dallas.
Q. What about Spiro?
A. When Spiro was asked about copying Maureen's Orr-Allee routine and write-up, he denied everything. That failing, he turned aggressive and frankly abusive. Threats followed, and in the end, he was given the choice of resignation or being fired. Spiro's going-away party was on the day after Spiro

left. At the party, consensus held that Spiro's departure was an addition by subtraction.

Q. What about the others?

A. Surprisingly, Jane came around. At first, she was openly antagonistic toward Maureen, but Maureen's hard work turned Jane into a Maureen cheerleader. Jane never owned up to the plagiarism and Gladys and Della never changed their minds about Maureen, though.

Q. Did Jenny walk?

A. Jenny stayed for a couple months after her interview and then left for a job in an LA suburb. A friend who stayed in touch reported that Jenny still thought that wearing the latest fashions and dating handsome guys were her top priorities, but she had become more introspective. It seems likely that she'll end up in the front office of an engineering contract operation. Unless a premium grade sugar daddy appears, of course.

Q. Did Bernie become open to hiring women as leaders?

A. Not really. He allowed Jane LaPlain to be an interviewee but doubled back down by demanding that John hire Jenny for all the wrong reasons.

Lesson 13.3: What is the biggest barrier to women like Maureen? The establishment's belief that once a secretary, always a secretary.

Chapter 14

A Hard Look at the Peter Principle
and a Glance
at the
Dilbert Principle

The managers in this book make errors at every turn, but despite all their missteps, they just keep blundering along. Surely, you'd think, some would be overwhelmed by futility. But no, on this third rock from the sun, things don't work that way. Despite all the errors they make and the flak they take, managerial attitudes remain regal. That is, once a king, always a king[67], and once a manager, always a manager.

This is as described by Peter. According to the Peter Principle[68] (PP), employees are promoted based on their successes in previous jobs until they reach a level at which they are no longer competent. And there they stay, for the rest of their careers.

The stock explanation for the PP phenomenon is that skills in one job may not translate to another job. For reasons to be presented below, we think this explanation glosses over underlying problems. But whatever our opinion, surely the issue warrants closer examination.

---

[67] The uncorrupted maxim is "Once a king, always a king, but once a knight is enough for any man."
[68] The Peter Principle. Peter, Laurence J. and Hull, Raymond. *The Peter Principle*, William Morrow & Co Inc, 1969 (Pan Books edition 1970).

While the PP is frequently observed in education and is present in every field, it's most easily studied in for-profit big business management where both organizational structure and performance are well documented in a formal manner. It's remarkable that the PP phenomenon persists in the for-profit setting despite concerns for the bottom line and the extensive resources expended in continued training precisely aimed at improving the skills of the weaker managers. It's a wonder how these people can be so resistant to becoming better managers.

In Lieu of a Case Study, our relevant experience

When we were promoted into management in a large, multi-national company, we were sent to a series of week-long Beginning Management (BM) classes. Added to our cohort of a dozen newly anointed were four well-established, veteran managers. The reason(s) for adding these four to our class was never publicly admitted, but their presence in our class was implicitly remedial BM training.

We all knew they were famed as jerks in social settings and contrarians as collaborators. Rumor held that they were painful to work for and stressful to supervise. Every year, their staff turnovers were among the highest in the company. On the per dollar budget and per employee bases, their business units were repeatedly among the least productive in the entire company.

But these bad managers were BM stars in our class. They made us newbies seem pitiful on every question because the veteran four knew ALL the correct answers.

The remedial training must have been helpful in some regards, but five, ten, and fifteen years later, these same guys were still in charge of the same work groups and their groups were still ranked among the ten most miserable work locales in the entire company.

We conclude that for at least these four guys, the remedial BM training was learned but not applied. So, not only do the skills in one job fail to translate to another job but even hammered-in management precepts may still fail to translate into appropriate management actions. Regardless of why it was, the PP held.

Let's conjecture regarding the above. In our heart of hearts, we believe that overall, managers are smart people who are lifetime learners. The message above, though, is that we have learned nothing by just looking at the managers' overalls. We'll have to get into their underalls to understand how they failed to apply the lessons they seemed to learn so well. And, of course, checking underalls is always a messy task.

At this point, the insightful reader will ask the obvious question: Why didn't senior management just replace these losers with competent managers? The obvious answer is that the managers of the failing managers were also operating at their level of incompetence.

Lesson 14.1: Incompetent managers find it difficult to admit to their mistakes and even more difficult to take steps to correct their mistakes.

In general, why do failing guys just keep on managing instead of recognizing their inadequacies and for their own peace of mind, go back to doing what they once did so well? We think that:

- The short answer is that they don't realize that they are failing.
- The slightly longer short answer is that they get a buzz out of telling others what to do.
- A somewhat longer short answer is that somehow taking the oath of management office causes their lifetime learner chip to rust.
- Our longest short answer is that after extensive research, we conclude that their learning chip isn't just rusted; it's corroded. These guys want the money and don't give a rip about whether they are good at managing. Further, someone above them in the food chain is also convinced that managing well doesn't matter.
- As we expected since we are examining underalls, the long answers are messy:

  Maybe it's because managers enjoy managing so much. They have no longing for the sense of honorable accomplishment arising from doing good work in the trenches. If so, this is a powerful testimonial on behalf of the management life. Tolling of the great BS bell in the sky all but drowns out this explanation, though.

Perhaps the manager knows he has lost his edge in his field of mastery and is wise enough to avoid reengaging when he knows he won't be able to cut it beside the freshly trained. For him, fear of proving to the world that he is technically obsolete trumps the disgrace of managing poorly. That, and managing pays better.

The obverse side of this lost-edge coin is that it's more likely that managers who are failures in management but refuse to go back to what they did well can't remember what it was that they did well.

Viewing the question as being a public health matter leads to a completely different explanation. Since we often observe that an incompetent senior manager has a cluster of incompetent junior managers reporting to him, perhaps incompetence is like stupidity. That is, it's infectious, like intelligence. What if some sort of slow virus or even a prion is the underlying cause of incompetence? Were this the case, instead of calling in a latter-day Peter Drucker[69], we'll need to alert the Center for Disease Control in Atlanta and sanction vaccine development work. The thought of a vaccine to prevent stupidity would surely alarm the anti-vaccers, though.

---

[69] Peter Drucker once put out management fires like Red Adair's cavalry put out oil well fires.

What can we do about this Peter Principle quandary?

We'd really like to find a way to help here because it's unfortunate for the managers, the people who work with them and for them, and for their organization. The only winners are their competitors. But we doubt there exist resolutions to situations where the managers are in place and their careers plateaued as a result of the Peter Principle in action.

We can't do diddly after the manager is in place. What about preempting the problem by selecting promotion candidates more thoughtfully?

A possibly useful analogy can be found in basketball. Gregg Popovich, Phil Jackson, Pat Summitt, and Mike Krzyzewski were all good college players, but far more successful as coaches than as players. Elgin Baylor, Ervin Johnson, Larry Bird, and Kareem Jabbar were tremendous college and pro players but at best so-so as coaches. In fact, it is widely accepted that because of their tremendous egos and their reliance on physical skills, the best players do not make good coaches.

Beyond their egos getting in the way, a reason offered for this disconnect is that the physically gifted athletes can star without being students of the game. They can afford to disdain X and O concerns because their physical skills and inherent talents overwhelm everything else.

The less talented warm the bench watching the games unfold and then they live in the tape replay room, sweating details and learning the nuances; if they don't learn the finer points, they don't play at all. Their big reward comes later because their studies puts them into position to instruct others on the intricacies of the game.

A player can't be coached to be taller or quicker. In general, talent and physical abilities can be polished but cannot be implanted if absent, so these characteristics are non-coachable. However, if the motivated player has the intelligence and analytical skills, in-depth understanding of game nuances can be implanted and polished by coaching.

So how does basketball figure into selecting managers? Let's think about this vis-à-vis selection of candidates for management positions. We know that if we select top performers to be new managers, we'll lose these performers' contributions. We don't know if these top performers can broaden their skills enough to meet the needs of their new higher-level positions and/or coach their subordinates into being top performers.

We want the newly ordained manager to coach (teach) subordinates about how to perform assigned tasks very well. That is, we want a task performance teacher rather than a task performer. So, instead of selecting candidates who crank out the best work, let's select candidates who are the most likely to teach their subordinates how to crank out the best work.

To select the candidates who are most likely to be good teachers, we need to scrutinize the reasons why the candidates have done so well at their current jobs. Do their analytical, problem solving, communication, and team collaboration skills set them apart? Or are they exceptionally fast learners? Did they bring a ton of relevant experience to the assignment, so they know just what to do when glitches arise? Is it because they have excellent motor skills or hand/eye coordination? Or maybe they are so smart or just work harder than others all day, every day.

We do not want a newly ordained manager whose only strength is producing a dazzling number of cubic yards of work per day, so let's divide success-driving factors into teachable and non-teachable characteristics. Teachable factors can be shared, but non-teachable factors remain unique to the individual possessing them.

Teachable skills that lead to high productivity:

Analytical -- these can be identified early on and groomed through experience and formal training. Most tech and hardware-oriented candidates have been relatively good analysts in their post-womb era.
On the downside, some get so immersed in the jargon and tech details that they can't explain the issues to anyone except themselves.

Problem solving — these can be advanced and refined with experience and by training programs. There are many "Problem Solving Training" courses available on the internet, and while their contents tend to overlap, these courses are indeed useful.

Communication — teachers need to communicate well. This is particularly important in highly specialized areas of technology and medicine where specialized terminology often inhibits effective communication. Workers can be trained in languages.

Understanding people — empathy and understanding others' personnel level problems is often a shortfall for the high-ego, super hard-working employee. Training in strategies for dealing with personnel conflicts is available and can be quite useful, provided the candidate does in fact have a functional empathy chip.

Ability to stay calm and carry on — this is a self-confidence issue that can be coached through practice and simulation. Giving the manager a menu of options for dealing with dilemmas and crises will bolster confidence.

Non-teachable characteristics for high productivity:

Extensive relevant experience — we can buy experience by hiring veteran workers, but we cannot confer it.

Fast work style — we think the ability to do work quickly and still make few errors is a function of worker ability to maintain focus on task. This is good for productivity but bad for leadership and communication because these workers focus by ignoring what's going on around them and ignoring the people around them, too.

We've had little success with teaching slow workers to move more quickly; they just made their mistakes faster. And we've had zero success in getting high-ego, monomaniacal workers to pay attention to what others are doing, thinking, or saying.

Quick hands, intelligence, visual acuity, hand/eye coordination — we doubt that anyone can teach a clumsy guy with coarse hands to do fine touch work. We can't teach a guy with the shakes how quit shaking, either, and great hand/eye coordination is a talent possessed only by a few.

Exceptional dedication to task — we hold doubts about the role model and leadership value of sanctimonious types who believe all about them are slackers. While we have been able to jack up motivation in workers who were less than totally dedicated, this lasted only until they knew we weren't watching.

Having a good eye for what's right and what's wrong — having a "feel" for what's right or wrong about performing a task is very useful, but not at all easy to convey to others. Some workers have a wonderful gut sense about their assignments, but we've never been able to teach anyone how to have good instincts.

The bottom line

Without remediation before the inept manager is put in place, the PP will raise its ugly head and the manager will remain a paragon of incompetency far into the future. We wish to avoid advancing candidates whose high productivity is the result of non-teachable characteristics.

So, we think it would be useful to select management candidates based on teachable skills rather than based on overall performance, in the hope that the selected candidates will be able to reproduce and groom their productive traits in subordinates.

Management selection efforts routinely examine the candidates' skill profiles. We are advocating carrying this skill profile assessment a step further by systematically excluding candidates whose high productivity can be attributed to non-teachable work characteristics. This will have two repercussions:

a) Excluding strong employees from management promotion consideration because they have a special talent or work very hard work will cause frustration. An unhappy hard-working, high performer may evolve into a misguided over-achiever and cause a mother of all headaches.

b) Appropriately rewarding the non-promotable top performer might run afoul compensation guidelines. Further, these non-promotable, high-performing, butt-busters often have outsized egos and see the world with tunnel vision. Being blinded to the picture outside of their fiefdom, it won't be easy to convince these insular workers that they are way better off by not being promoted into management.

We think these concerns are lesser problems for the organization than making the grievous error of promoting a top performer into his level of incompetency.

Lesson 14.2: It's preferable to select promotion candidates based on their teachable skills rather than based on their overall job performance.

The Dilbert Principle

We can't leave the Peter Principle without considering the Dilbert Principle (DP); that "the most ineffective workers will be systematically moved to the place where they can do the least damage — management".

If we may change the "will be" in the above to "should be", this is an utterly charming and clearly sensible business strategy. Even after discounting for mirth's value and cynicism's merit, it's obvious that the DP is truth.

But where? We believe the DP is operative in settings where employee termination for poor performance is very difficult, such as with tenured university faculty or in the Federal Civil Service. Inept, careless, and obsolete professors are indeed quietly but deliberately shunted into administration jobs to get them out of the classroom. In the Civil Service, where a manager's attempts to fire a dud subordinate puts the manager at greater hazard of termination than the subordinate, the widely (and openly) accepted strategy of choice is kicking the loser upstairs.

In business settings, we've seen a few managers get shunted into dotted box jobs with no real responsibilities, but we cannot recall ever observing a failing subordinate overtly moved into management to get him out of the way of the productive workers. So, either the DP is rarely operative in businesses, or more likely, it's artfully concealed.

The DP simply must be present in business settings because the concept is too close to truth. So why are we not seeing this? We think these explanations are logical:

Many managers fail to recognize their subordinates' shortcomings because the managers themselves are incompetent by reason of the PP.

Many managers do recognize their subordinates' shortcomings but underestimate the value of moving the subordinates into jobs the subordinates could do well.

A substantial portion of managerial tasks are in fact administrative busywork that could be performed in an adequate manner by a subpar subordinate. This is news the typical manager will not want to share.

Many managers badly overvalue the skills needed to perform their managerial tasks and badly underestimate the ability of subordinates to perform these managerial tasks.

As an example, men are prone to think that the "men's jobs" they are performing are so difficult and require so much skill that the lion's share of tasks are beyond the reach of women. But consider how men drivers once disparaged the competence of women drivers—in our current circumstances, half the nation would be either home-schooled or illiterate if we didn't have women driving school buses.

Chapter 15

Simple Solutions — Complex Issues
and Other Oxymorons

This book, like all such books, needs a place to dump issues that actually matter but can't be shoehorned in elsewhere. Most books use the last chapter to tie up these loose ends, but our last chapter is a review and the next-to-last chapter is about closing out careers so that has to stay put, too. So, be forewarned. This is the stash-the-crap chapter.

Simple answers to everything

Are there simple ways to make complex personnel decisions? Sure. But do these simple ways lead to correct decisions? Well -- nothing ventured, nothing lost, so let's see how things turn out for simple approaches to staff selection, culling, and retention decisions. That is, selecting new employees, writing tickets out of town for losers, retaining good employees and retrieving good employees who have fallen on hard times.

Our Bernie advocated doing things the simple way, so we'll ask, "What would Bernie do?" We'll look at what he and his subordinates did and think of what might have been.

Case Study

Bernie was an old-school manager with strongly held beliefs. His creed was that every question that mattered had a simple answer and every regulation that regulated him was flawed. His management of crises was always quick and sure; he'd preempt the crisis de jour by causing a worse one. Although he'd pursue any ploy leading to a cheapskate solution, Bernie had ethics—if by chance, the expedient way was the correct way, he'd be the first in line to insist that things be done properly.

Bernie did lots of things at DA just because he could do lots of things. There was a web of consistency in his personnel policies, though:

His hiring selection strategy?
Find a couple guys who come close to meeting the minimal job specs and hire the one willing to accept the low-ball offer.

His staff retention policies?
Raises? "The top-end staff guys always get raises. We start with the Cost of Living (CoL) index increase and then beef that up by 0.1%. We can set aside the big bucks for these raises because everybody but the top two or three guys in the department are already overpaid. The premium feature in our plan is that raises will not be rescinded if the CoL goes down."

Promotions? "YOU want a promotion?"—snort, pause, chuckle— "If you're half as good as you think you are, quit. Today. You'll have a job offer from somewhere else by noon tomorrow and get your pick of offers by the end of the week."

Advanced training? "Huh? You want OUR support for advanced degree training so YOU qualify for a promotion?" —long pause, with eye roll— "If we ever need a guy with an advanced degree, I'll hire him."

Sick leave? "You're not in the ICU, you haven't called hospice, and you think you should get **sick** leave?" —sigh, with steepled fingers— "Besides the note from your Mommy, you'll need a comprehensive statement from the doctor. That's **our** doctor. He's in Vegas. Should be back in a month or two."

Compassion? "He died? So that's why he wasn't at work today! Gee. Didn't know he was sick. Got a death certificate?" "Funeral? Time off with pay is only for funerals of immediate family. That's HR policy. Just take vacation." "You have a 'life-crisis'?" —grunt, pause, grunt— "Too bad. This makes you a security risk. Rules are rules, so we'll have to let you go."

A problem employee? First, find (and should none be found, then create) some firing-cause-quality dirt on this loser. Second, get a buddy who owes you a big favor to sign an affidavit swearing that the dirt is fact. Third, use the dirt to justify firing the loser. Fourth, (with wide smile) "If the cited dirt is proven fraudulent, your buddy is already set up to take the fall, and who cares if the loser sues? The company has lots of lawyers—they don't have that much to do."

Any other HR questions?

Blow off the HR goals and quotas, tell that whining ombudsman to go to hell, and disregard everything else.

How could Bernie be this way? Easy. Bernie landed contracts that kept the wolf from the door at DA. He was the rainmaker. Further, his contract oversight provided him **alone** with a map showing every corporate closet that held a skeleton. That made him an even bigger threat to senior management than to his subordinates, so whatever he chose to do, he did. As he mellowed, though, he found he had more fun if he made others do the set-up work on personnel manipulation. So, Bernie assigned accountability (but not authority) for all salaried, non-managerial personnel actions to the management trio of Cy, Lawrence, and John. Non-managerial inputs to personnel decisions and actions were invariably welcomed and then invariably ignored.

For jobs above the clerical levels, Bernie routinely vetoed hiring of minorities and all women he deemed to be unattractive. So, the management troika preempted Bernie's vetoes by interviewing only white males. After the interviews for an opening were completed, each manager carefully reviewed the other managers' interview notes and then chose the 2 candidates he thought were the best. A consensus ranking of these 2 to 6 candidates came out of a managers' closed-door, transcript-free meeting. The central issues at these consensus meetings were the managers' gut feelings about the candidates' attitudes, and, to a lesser extent, how the candidates would fit into the department's staffing needs. The job was offered to the first ranked guy. If he didn't take it, the second ranked guy got the offer. If the second guy also turned down the offer, it was back to the drawing board.

The managers' collaborative process worked well; out of their first nine hires, all but Abie were heavy hitters. The tenth hire was the CEO's namesake grandson Durwood (aka Little Dimwood). When Li'l Dimmy failed to make even one manager's short list, Bernie used executive privilege. Li'l Dimmy stepped in the door as a neo-incompetent, within a month on the job had mastered global incompetence, and even more impressively, the Thursday Night Office Bowling Team TWICE voted him Fool of The Month.

When Lawrence started the termination process for Li'l Dimmy, Bernie undermined the proceedings. In a rare show of courage, Lawrence wouldn't knuckle under. Bernie "compromised" by privately arranging to have Dimmy kicked upstairs into a better job in an enemy's department. Bernie then publicly trashed his three managers' hiring process.

After taking particular umbrage with decisions based on the managers' gut instincts, Bernie slipped away for training at a weeklong **"Get in Touch with Your Inner Cosmos"** charm farm program at a swankish ranch just outside of Santa Fe.

Get in Touch... was a self-awareness retreat featuring fine wines, a gourmet menu, dimmed lights, shuttered windows, monotone lectures, and soft, rhythm-free elevator music[70]. The trainees were seated in the lotus position, wearing blindfolds. They were gagged with mouthpieces to

---

[70] John knew all these key facts because his friend Janitor Jim pilfered a course brochure from the top of Della's desk.

muffle their voices, lest someone spoke aloud and broke the trance so very necessary for hearing viscera.

The following Monday, at a special management shaft meeting, Bernie bubbled in exultation about his training. He had ascended to a higher level of understanding and declared that he was now one of the rare mortals who had "truly climbed the mountain and heard his inner voice[71]". Just how far Bernie delved into his psyche was unclear. The testimonials in the class brochure were murky, too, but John guessed there were other things about **Get in Touch...**, such as faculty credentials and the purported versus real value of the training, that were far murkier.

Bernie began implementation of **Get in Touch...** the very next morning, for he was in touch with his inner self and in turn, his self was in touch with the universe. Henceforth, he would make all important decisions. The lotus position was cast aside along with the gags, masks, muted lights and soothing sounds. His implementation message was simple:

"Everybody! I'm in charge here, and I hear my guts."

For Bernie, it was a whole new era. He updated his policies to incorporate his gut instinct. Henceforth, he'd hire the cheapest guy who met most of the job specs and didn't nauseate him. Just bring the problem and people before him, he'd ponder for a moment, and Bingo! The perfect solution. All would marvel at the wisdom of his gut.

Bernie had total faith in his gut instincts, but not even he dreamed they could be so effective so soon! Within one

---

[71] Bernie was no doubt speaking from the heart, but by sheer coincidence the brochure happened to use these phrases, as in "Become one of the one-in-a-million who has truly climbed the mountain and heard his inner voice."

hour of his announcement, every personnel complaint on file at HR had been withdrawn, every conflict resolved, every gripe ungripped, and every bicker turned to a coo. All things bad had vanished into dark corners.

Bernie chose to believe that this sudden improvement could be attributed to his wisdom. "Morale has never been better! Everyone is so sure of success that conflicts have all gone away!" he boasted. Indeed, all the employees were suddenly hard at work with their heads down. Only faceless cynics believed that the conflict was quelled by the fear of being the first to bare his issue before Bernie's desk.

The three managers persuaded Bernie that gut instinct would fail as a guiding beacon on engineering and computer issues. Bernie insisted on calling the shots with the touchy-feely stuff, such as hiring and firing and adjudicating employee conflicts, though.

Happily for the managers, all the touchy-feely stuff had been banished in that first remarkable hour. Unhappily for Bernie, after those first few moments of joy, he fell into despair because his most precious asset, his gut instincts, were unutilized and languishing. Fearing his insights might decay, he haunted the halls for needs for Solomonic wisdom.

Bernie's first chance to star came with one of Cy's guys, Jake. Jake was a good-enough engineer, but his best friend was a bottle. Jake had made it only to Step 2 at AA when his wife died. Depressed, Jake took unpaid leave and admitted himself to a rehab. Nothing was heard from him for weeks. Then, unexpectedly, Jake burst into work one Wednesday morning. Bubbling with enthusiasm, he exclaimed that he was ready to take on the world.

Cy was out of town on a Top-Secret foray. Eager to display his gut instincts, Bernie leaped into the vacuum, ordering Jake out of his old job, away from his two work buddies, and into the lead engineer slot on a huge, ultra-priority project. This mammoth step up in Jake's responsibility lasted for the rest of that day. On Thursday morning, Jake's daughter-in-law found Jake in the garage with the car's ignition still on. The farewell note said to call Cy, but with Cy incommunicado, the call was routed to Bernie.

It looked like the funeral should be on Monday. Ever gallant, Bernie told Jake's daughter-in-law that if she scheduled the funeral on Saturday, Jake's co-workers could attend. Bernie's "hands were tied" by the required case-by-case review of exceptions to the HR "immediate family only" reg on personal leave for funerals together with Bernie's policy forbidding vacation on Mondays unless scheduled two weeks in advance.

So, instead of using Jake's church on Monday, the funeral was in a dusty, broom closet-sized side chapel on Saturday. Bernie had a tee time and with Cy still out of touch, nobody else at DA or AA knew that Jake had died because the death notice was delayed until the Sunday newspaper. The sneezing hardly mattered and with only two attendees, the daughter-in-law and her sister, the size of the chapel was not a problem.

The sad thing was that David, who was Jake's only surviving[72] son, was an Army E-3 in Germany. He was about broke because returning to the States for his mother's funeral had cost a bundle. So, when his wife called him about his

---

[72] Jake, Jr. and Ronnie had been killed in Viet Nam.

dad's death, David hitched a ride back to the States on an Air Force plane. Engine problems forced the plane down at Gander. David arrived home late Sunday evening.

Bernie was not to be faulted about Jake's son missing his father's funeral, though. Nor did Bernie accept any responsibility for Jake's decision to end it all. "Actually, it all worked out," Bernie privately told Cy later, "if Jake hadn't killed himself, you would have had to let him go because with his mental problems, he might have become a security risk."

At DA, things fell right into place — Don, the temp who was filling in for Jake, was switched to permanent status. The switch was by acclamation and rightly so; Don knew Jake's job and was a walk-on-water star. On behalf of his gut, Bernie claimed all the credit for choosing Don. This was notable since Bernie first met Don after HR had switched Don to permanent.

The next gut decision event came only a week or two later. Dallas had abruptly chosen to FSER[73] rather than face a DoD Review Board investigating "Quality Control (QC) Irregularities" on Dall's battery project. FSER was Dall's only realistic option — he was an okay engineer but the sloppiest dresser in the department and his QC records were almost as messy. He'd done nothing wrong except keep ragged records, but the DoD review Whip & Thumbscrew Storage Vaults in the headquarters building were opened the minute that the review was scheduled.

Since being innocent has never been a defense at a DoD Review, Dall's only chance was for Bernie to intervene. If Bernie would just promise to upgrade departmental QC

---

[73] FSER: Fall on the Sword of Early Retirement.

record checking and storage processes, the DoD guy said he'd call off the dogs.

Bernie wanted a better dressed guy in Dall's job slot, though, so Dall went under the bus. To refill Dall's slot, Bernie called HR about on-file applications. What he asked for was unclear, but he stated that the woman who screened applications said, "Jerry looked good". She must have been taken by Jerry's picture because his credentials were pitiful.

In any case, Jerry was Bernie's first interviewee and Jerry looked good to Bernie, too, because Bernie aborted the hiring process by telling Jerry during the interview that he had already won the job.

Bernie informed the staff that his gut instinct was correct again. "Jerry is THE guy," he declared. "More interviews would be a waste of my valuable time."

The three managers were dismayed; Bernie had given Jerry a pass on his sub-mediocre academic performance at a third-rate school and had ignored the oh-so-delicate wording in both of Jerry's two letters of recommendation.

So, Jerry the peacock was duly hired. Although peacocks in general know little about engineering, almost any zoo or even common street peacock would have been a better hire than Jerry. Jerry was one of these unique guys who does little, still gets it all wrong, and along the way he pisses off all about him to the extent that their productivity falls off, too.

Bernie went through the full denial-to-defensive-to-confrontational rage routine with all who bore bad news about Jerry, so it took a full four[74] months before Bernie got

---

[74] All new hires were on probationary status for three months. During this time, termination could be without cause and was fairly easy. After 90 days, terminations required cause and heavy documentation.

pressed into the candor corner. He hadn't really listened to his gut, he said. Jerry had looked too much like a Marine, and Bernie loved that Marine look. "Jerry was dressed and groomed so well that it distracted me from my gut instinct."

An instant later, though, the wrath of Bernie reemerged and any hope of firing Jerry vanished. "This organization has one desperate need," Bernie fumed, "you people have got to buff up your slovenly image. You come to work dressed like you're homeless. You wear sport coats instead of suits to work! You have ratty shaves and your white shirts have yellow armpits. Your suit pants have shining seats. There's no linen in your breast pockets, if you do own any cuff links they are crappy filled gold, you can't tie a Windsor knot and then you get the tie crooked besides..."

In mid-September, Cy fired Milt for smoking in the flammable storage area. Milt was a temporary and a non-security-cleared gofer, so Cy moved to refill the opening with another temp. Unfortunately, Jerry's continued failings gave Bernie a gnawing need to prove to the world that his was the wisest gut after all, so he preempted Cy and offered Derek a permanent job without interviewing anybody. How Bernie came to have a permanent opening and have Derek's application in hand was a mystery.

On his second day, Derek came to work drunk and crashed a loaded forklift into a bank of shelving. The shelving was "full of tons of test equipment, so anchors weren't needed". The shelves tipped like dominos. The damages ran into the hundreds of thousands.

Bernie rushed to the warehouse and was greeted by Derek's vigorous explanation of why it wasn't his fault.

Lesson 15.1: As a general rule, if you are drunk and have done something stupid, it's a good idea to keep your mouth shut.

Remark: It's always a bad idea to get in your boss' boss' face when only a 100% mouth breather with Stage 6 Alzheimer's and a lethal-quality head cold could miss the smell of booze on your breath. And it's not clever at all to explain how it was another guy's fault when you were alone in the building and the guy you blame was on vacation that day.

When the managers as a group confronted Bernie about the unfortunate decision to hire Derek, Bernie only mumbled and made his chair squeak. He finally admitted that he'd gotten Derek's application from "a friend" and mistook this Derek for another Derek with the same name. This other Derek had played college football, so Bernie's gut told him that Derek surely would be an excellent permanent employee. This justification was remarkably fanciful since this Derek was about 5-8 and 140 pounds while the football Derek had been a left tackle.

In any case, Bernie quietly withdrew his gut instinct mandate and eventually put the trio of managers back in charge of recruiting. They went back to their own process.

Discussion of Case Study

Simplification of hiring

Hiring Derek was simple stupidity plus carelessness, while Bernie's hiring of Jerry is worth examining. When Bernie was faced with selecting from a stack of applications, he cut to the chase. He chose the guy who looked like a

Marine poster model and later blamed HR. "HR made the mistake. They told me that Jerry was their choice."

Had Bernie compared Jerry's resumé with his recommendation letters, even Bernie might have surmised that the man depicted by the resumé was created by an imaginative resumé author. So, if indeed Bernie wanted a fictional character on staff, a far more cost-effective move would have been to put the imaginative writer on retainer.

Bernie preempted the management team and simply picked the guy who dressed well. Bernie made the mistake, but the managers had to correct things. This was unfair; Bernie hired Jerry, and Bernie should have had to fire Jerry or at least sanction Jerry's dismissal.

Lesson 15.2: Let he who hires the loser, fire the loser.

Bernie couldn't be bothered by reading lots of applications, but you won't have that luxury. You won't have to bust your butt finding the absolutely toppanotcha applicant, though, because the highly motivated fast learner usually outshines the ultra-profile star over the long haul.

You'll have lots of ways to select via credentials, but all are flawed:

- Relevant experience is the easily justified, minimal flak approach. The risk is that it makes what he has done more important than what he is going to do.
- Training can predict upward potential but shows little about future productivity.

- Letters of recommendation are helpful **ONLY IF** you can trust the letter writers. Remember that the applicant gets to choose his references. Old friends will lie a little and managers hoping to get rid of a loser will lie a lot.

- Resumés, CVs, and letters of recommendation stress the applicant's positives and downplay the negatives. So, as with all hedged statements, what's not stated is more important than what's stated.

A reasonable strategy is to discount the positives and focus on what's missing. But how do you know what's not there? You'll need a checklist detailing everything that you'd expect to learn from the guy's credentials. Creating your first checklist won't be easy, but it's an investment that can be reused in many interviews. One way to create this checklist is to amalgamate the chronologies, extracurricular interests, related training, volunteer work, ill-fated ventures, and whatever else is reported by many applicants. You'll want to find what A is not reporting but B, C, D, and/or F are reporting. If nothing else, having a checklist like this will suggest potential topics for grilling in later interviews.

- Or, you can blithely toss the credentials aside and wing it. Ignoring HR's rules and quotas is loads of fun, but one day you will be invited to the HR woodshed — where you may be persuaded to hire the "you WILL hire him" HR nominee.

Bernie was not at peril of the HR woodshed. You will be, though. Let us suppose you dutifully dig through the pile of CVs and resumés and reduce the stack to a prime few by comparing experience, training, skill sets, growth potential, and whatever else floats your boat. You interview the few and find two or more applicants who meet your objective specs. It's time to think about subjective criteria. It's time to listen to your gut.

Gut sense issues

Gut sense is a wonderful thing. But most managers who think they have it do not. And, since we suspect we're short on gut sense, too, we sure don't know how to tell others how to get it. We know of two attributes to evaluate by gut sense, though.

Attitude

Bernie assumed all his employees had a positive attitude about their work and the company. This must have been true; if not, they would have left long before. Bernie got excited only about bad attitude and that was only as dirt to justify a firing.

In the minds of the trio of managers, attitude was the single most important employee issue. They saw it as a complicated matter that was much more than just a can-do mindset. Their opinions on attitude can be summarized as follows:

Attitude depends on the individual's self-confidence, a willingness to collaborate, to persevere, and to put the assignment needs ahead of needs for personal gain. The worker needs to want to learn what doing the job well entails and with that knowledge, to do the job well. It's enthusiasm without rah-rah-rah; it's bravery without the need to be known as brave. The stickiest point of all is that what's good varies; what an R&D science interviewer takes as cheap swagger, marketing types see as laudable and even necessary self-confidence. Positive attitude is hard to quantify, and that alone is enough to make it a gut judgment call.

Candidate fit in the organization

The three managers agreed that every working environment has a set of characteristics that determine how and how well the work gets done. Regardless of how clever and well-qualified an employee might be, if the employee doesn't fit into the environment, failure will follow. It's unclear why some people are good at fitting in while others are not, so sensing this trait surely calls for a gut instinct evaluation.

Hearing the gut's advice

Hearing the gut clearly is not easy if the candidate's credentials have special distinctions or flaws (the halo/horns effect). Trophy hires are wondrous, but do the expected gains exceed the expected costs? Ordinary hires come with lower expectations but require less maintenance and some turn out very well.

Most of the time, though, hearing the gut simply requires setting aside prejudices and believing the facts. As in Don's case, hiring decisions driven by clear and positive evidence typically result in incremental staff additions.

The gut speaks softly and gets drowned out by distractions. At the Santa Fe charm school, they handicapped the senses to avoid distractions. Bernie was sure that he was always too strong to be distracted, but he was wrong about that, too. Dallas was a good-enough engineer, but Bernie was distracted by appearances. Thus, the dumbass mistake of replacing messy by incompetent. Hiring Jerry to replace Dallas was a decremental staff addition.

And finally, Derek was an excremental addition to the staff. The three managers agreed that there is need to be careful about which sector of the gut is heard. If Bernie had indeed been listening to his gut when he decided to hire Derek, the only plausible explanation was that the rectal orifice segment was doing the talking.

Lesson 15.3: When you listen to your gut, you gotta be careful about which sector of your gut is doing the talking.

Problem employees

Every organization is stocked with a few staff members with quirks that aggravate their colleagues. Being oblivious to complainers and identifying with jerks, Bernie's hiring policies failed to screen out almost any grade of loser. As a result, Bernie's staff tended to be above-average in below-average staff.

Jerks

Some guys seem to have malware on their hard drive. The three managers were acutely aware that jerks are typically unpleasant to have as coworkers, but managing them is worse, and being managed by a jerk is still worse. That's understandable, what with Bernie being their boss. Further, they feared that jerks in charge are jerks in perpetuity.

So, our three were more wary of jerks than most. In fact, the three quietly screened for jerks during their interview process. Here's how they did it:

If the managers agreed that the guy was acting as a jerk during his interviews, the guy was ALWAYS dropped from the list of candidates. But jerks don't act as jerks all the time. So, during the interviews, the managers routinely checked for significant aggression, belligerence, dogmatism, and otherisms. The signs and symptoms of the jerk syndrome were carefully recorded, discussed, and adjudicated.

If the interviewee was suspected to be a latent jerk in stealth mode, they gave him a chance to be a jerk during the interview and watched if he ran with it. They asked him what annoyed him. Since there were no rules about such in those days, they allowed the conversation to drift into special interests — politics, immigration, the Second Amendment, religion, hobbies, and whatever other axes the interviewee had to grind. They asked him about pet peeves and how he dealt with workplace conflict. They asked how he'd respond if someone figured out how to push his buttons.

They got rises out of most of the interviewees with these questions. The few who went ballistic were assiduously excluded from further consideration.

Since a jerk is in his natural state most of the time and if in stealth mode, can often be coaxed out into the open, the three managers' jerk screen usually worked out okay for candidates for subordinate jobs. It's way harder, though, to ensure that your potential supervisor is not a jerk. It will be a challenge to introduce "Are you a jerk?" probes when the potential supervisor is running the interview, and even if you do get to pose your queries, he might not answer the questions. Asking the hosting HR will be like asking the mother of a serial murdering rapist if her son is a good man, but gingerly exploring the issues with your potential cohorts might be useful. At worst, you'll have a better shot at getting your "Is he a jerk?" questions asked in discussions with potential colleagues.

Complainers

The subordinates who whined about everything and bellyached about everybody pained their colleagues but caused no worries for the three managers. The managers knew it was just the complainers' ways of showing that they were happy. It's well known that bellyachers have deep inner needs to kvetch. Forcing their fellow employees to listen to insults and woes may be the only joy the whiners can extract from life.

The staff who had to work near chronic whiners did merit special concern, though. Graciously putting up with a colleague's non-stop bitching is a marketable skill that is easily noted and merits reward. The reward may well be a different and better job for the gracious. You'll want to ensure that the rewarded job is one that you, not someone else, chooses.

But if the whiner gets to be too much for his fellow employees to endure, it's time for you to go nuclear. He'll claim you don't **listen** to him. So, stop ignoring his complaints. Pay attention to him. Pay way too much attention to him.

Turn his idle bitching into ugly, hard work—make him put his grievances into writing. Then make him provide evidence for every grubby little whine. And then require him to propose a solution to every damn one. These solutions should be in minute detail, with action items—the whole nine yards. Finally, gather him and all affected parties in a conference room and start with his least significant gripe. Spend no less than a full hour ripping apart his evidence and his proposed solution(s) to his most minimal complaint. It won't be pleasant for you and it may be intolerable for the poor folks he complains about, but he'll get the message. He might even quit. Gee. Wouldn't that be too bad?

Lesson 15.4: Rank has its privileges. The boss can always be a bigger pissant than the subordinate.

Losers

Losers are incompetent by choice as often as by ability. Labor union guys claim it's all management's fault, while management claims it's solely a worker problem. The real truth lies somewhere in between, but no matter what, as the first line supervisor, it's up to you to fix things. And you might be able to fix it, because jacking up worker motivation almost always jacks up performance. Most supervisors jack up worker motivation by kicking ass.

In some cases, training works, too. Many workers can be trained to do better, although you'll have to view your effort as an investment. Training for the lower end guys is at best a wash when compared to benefit gained, e.g., see complainer fix above. For the bottom few, miracles will not happen. Unlimited correction doesn't cure stupidity and bad judgment is pretty much irreparable. For these bottom dwellers, Moh's Law of Personnel Performance Entropy applies – while you can't fix many performance problems, you can always make the problems worse. The good news is that worsening the problem might give you sufficient ammunition for firing the guy.

Retaining Personnel

Bernie claimed that troubled staff members were always increased security risks. He also enjoyed terminating employees who were not performing exceptionally well at the time, regardless of their prior track records. So, since citing increased security risk hazard was a legal and nearly foolproof way to justify a dismissal, retaining troubled staff members in the face of Bernie's overblown security risk claims was the trickiest part of the managers' jobs.

Retaining depressed workers

The three managers condemned Bernie as callous in Jake's situation. Granted, Bernie may not have known that Jake was hanging on the edge, but Bernie treated Jake's family in a shabby manner.

Lesson 15.5: If you have a guy who has had the desperate blues almost forever but suddenly perks up and says he's ready to take on the world, WORRY about him.

Remark: After Jake did himself in, the managers read up on the issue and found that paradoxically, guys who are depressed are often saved by their depression. The deeply depressed simply don't have enough energy to kill themselves. So, if a manager finds that his guy has a burst of energy after suddenly emerging from a very dark place, this can be a sign that the guy has turned a corner in his mind and made the dreaded key decision.

Lesson 15.6: Don't pile work onto someone coming back from a depression time out.

Remark: Particularly if he says he wants challenging tasks. Give him a pleasant, light task to see how it goes. Make sure he has lots of kind, thoughtful, and above all stable people around him, night and day. Call for some easy intermediate deliverables as a way of keeping track of him. And the minute your meeting with him is over, call HR or his wife or his analyst or life coach or mother or somebody so that you aren't the only one who's to blame if bad comes down.

Finding the correct niche for the troubled employee

Bernie agreed with HR's contention that finding the correct niche for the troubled employee solved a lot of problems. Almost all of Bernie's correcting niches were far from Bernie in other departments, in other companies, or in unemployment lines, though.

Suppose you've tried at least a couple placements for a troublesome new guy, and no spot has worked at all. Dump him. Quickly. You'll be doing yourself a favor and giving him a favor. You carve out dead wood and he won't be wasting career years in a job that has no future for him. It's usually easy to dump a so-so new guy during the probationary period. Ascertain the time limit for your operation and be prepared to act decisively well before the probation period ends. It calls for a degree of ruthlessness to dump employees who might benefit from a second chance, but does the probation clock start over if you give the marginal guy a second chance? Ah, no. Giving a second chance is rarely a benefit for management and makes saying no harder when another dud wants a do over.

The issue above makes the easy-in, easy-out feature of temporary employees quite attractive. Many temps are compromised in some way, though, so you need to be wary about moving a temp into a permanent slot. On the plus side, with temps it's easy to observe work habits, attitude, and fit in the organization. You just have to make the effort to do it.

Retaining yourself

We will close this chapter with an issue that might cause your cheese to bind. When things go from bad to worse in your workplace, you might be tempted to bail out. This is a good idea more often than not, but if you are ambivalent about hanging around and trying to control the slide in the workplace, there are three things to remember:

— The guy with a plan almost always comes out of a skirmish in better shape than the guy who tries to wing it. Being a good guy is not a plan. Hope is not a plan. Prayer is not a plan. Get a plan.

— The rules governing your work won't get simpler.

— You can't go home. You can't turn the clock back, either, and you might not want to. In the cold gray light of dawn, if you look in the mirror and all you can see is a guy who is way past his prime, his prime wasn't all that great, either.

Chapter 16

End Game Management

Is your new boss the kind of guy who makes insufferable jerks seem okay, but his admin The Queen Cobra is way worse? Has not one thing about managing your crew gone okay for you since seems like forever? You say you've already changed everything about you, what you do, and how you do it? And—that—just—made—things–worse? If you could only find time to surf the net for the snake pit Help Wanted ads, you'd upgrade your job? Are your neurons so tangled that you can't even do Monday's Sudoku, let alone find a way out of your entrapment? Is that what's troublin' you, Bunky?

Well, be you a gaffer who has played out his hand or a younger, eager type who is currently drawing fire, it sounds like it's time for you to move on to something else or maybe bag it up forever. But in either case, you need a departure strategy. No strategy is foolproof, but just about any plan is better than no plan. You have several options:

a) You might want to sound the charge and write your own ticket out the door. This is a high return/high risk strategy that might win big, but it won't be easy to find something else you'd rather do that pays enough. Further, just fixing things enough to make them tolerable won't be okay; you'll want to make things way better.

b) You might want to just hang on because you're sure there will be sunnier weather ahead.

c) You might want to hang on and wait to be coaxed. Hoping for a lucrative buyout, are we? But what if the buyout turns into a sellout and you get an unwelcome invitation to the gilded halls? Where they give you no options except choosing between signing a letter of resignation that's effective that morning or listening to a hatchet man read a list of offenses and then being fired on the spot? Some report that being coaxed ruined their whole day.

d) Or, you might want to circle the wagons and fight. For how long, though? Until they force you to retire? Then what? Whine and grouse as they escort you out the door? Whining never helps and grousing every step of the way to the parking lot is scarcely better, but what if the grousing succeeds? Do you really want to die at work? Boots-on deaths are messy, and if you asked around, most employers would say that they'd much prefer that you took care of dying on your own time.

Agreed, your future's looking dim. Let's review the bidding. As stated earlier in this book, there are two legitimate reasons for wanting to be promoted into management.

The first is the textbook reason; you're sure you'll do the job well.

The second is the alternative. If you don't step up to the plate will you have to accept being managed by the scourge of the land?

Likewise, there are three valid reasons to stop managing.

The first is that if you don't step away, you'll get put away. If so, you'll want to retain as much control over your fate as possible.

The second valid reason seems blindingly obvious to everybody except those to whom it applies — hubris must be set aside. The conspicuous overachiever[75] Lee Iacocco said it best; "Lead, follow, or get out of the way."

The third reason is the distance to your horizon. This might be measured in time or difficulty of terrain, with the terrain the most important. Consider this: What if your failures had been booming successes instead? Would your boss have Jerry Jonesed[76] you by proclaiming to one and all that you and your staff did nothing more than you were paid to do? If so, you, and probably your staff as well, are forever screwed.

So, you think it's time for you to go out the door. What do you have to do?

1. Recheck to make sure that you really do have a problem.
2. Decide what you want to do with the rest of your life.
3. Ensure that you'll have food on the table and a roof over your head.

---

[75] "conspicuous overachiever" is an MBA term meaning "arrogant, glory-grabbing, and slave-driving son of a bitch".
[76] After the Jimmy Johnson-coached Dallas Cowboys won the Super Bowl, Jerry Jones told the world that Jimmy J was not needed; the Cowboys were so good that any coach would have won with that team.

4. Figure out who is going to be in charge after you are gone, and act wisely.
5. Take care of your staff, because they will likely be in for a hard time, too.

Okay, enough abstract crap. It's time for a Case Study. Consider the situation at Desert Aromatics (DA) on the morning when the years of plenty turned into the autumn of despair.

A Multi-Faceted Case Study

Our Guys (Lawrence, Cyrus, Maurice, and John) are all non-exceptional veteran managers. All earn a living wage, but raises have been trending downward toward token cost-of-livings. At DA, none will ever see another promotion. The headhunters haven't called in ages. Not one of Our Guys can remember the last time his name was listed among the company's rising stars. Their friends now whisper that none of Our Guys' names ever were. Even Lawrence, who always smiles, is unable to see a way to get from where he is to where he wants to be on the org chart.

Cy's and Lawrence's home mortgages are paid off, their kids are through college and earning their own living. Maurice lives in a house inherited by his wife and still denies that he's ever been a daddy. John is renting. His kids are teenagers and both need college money. All except Maurice have quit dreaming about being nineteen and horny. It's unclear how the wives feel about that, but that's their problem. Well, maybe that makes it Our Guys' problem, too, but that still doesn't make it our problem.

Life at DA has been okay until this morning, when a Mammoth Cave-sized chuckhole opened up in DA's yellow brick road. "Our Guys' Project", the Mark VIII Widget[77], has failed. The news was on TV. Up to yesterday, the Mark VIII was DA's hot new product. Sales projections were through the roof. Our Guys and all of their crews were working nights, weekends, and holidays on the Mark VIII. But now, with the breaking news of the prototype fraud on top of Lawrence's engineers failing to tweak production run Mark VIII units to perform even as well as the obsolete Mark VI, the Mark VIII sales won't cover the patent rights. The Mark VIII is not yet down the tube, but it's in the pot along with smelly brown things that most won't want to touch.

The company stock has crashed, and the once-distant rumblings of hostile takeover thunder are so close that you can smell the ozone. The DA Board of Directors called an emergency teleconference at 8 AM MDT.

Before 8:10, the CEO and his claque of toadies assured the Board that "Heads will roll!" and indeed, a head has already rolled. Bernie the Boss is now banished to a dotted box job with Della and one other report, Maurice.

Bernie's replacement is Englebert Zelle III (aka E. Zelle the Weazelle). He's a 29-year-old who flunked out of FBI training and is rumored to be the internal security snitch at DA. Trained as a lawyer and bean counter, E. Zelle thinks ASME Standards[78] are what the TSA uses for security line control at airports.

---

[77] Bernie described the Mark VIII Widget as "Mousetrap Maximus".
[78] ASME Standards: American Society of Mechanical Engineers Standards

Lesson 16.1: Senior managers like Bernie do not get fired for poor job performance. They get deposed when a higher power needs to demonstrate to a still higher power that "Steps are being taken to ensure …".

Heads are rolling, but Our Guys claim they are not at fault because they and their teams have given their all to the Mark VIII for close to five years. And besides, they didn't fail, their teams didn't fail, it was **the Mark VIII that failed**.

It's time for Our Guys to think again. There are lotsa becauses why they'll be blamed:

- Unlike Marketing or Product Design, development support work has zero cachet.
- Our Guys managed all the support work.
- Cy was the premier bad news messenger.
- So what if Maurice's manufacturing audits blew the whistle about assembly using uninspected minimum-bid components?
- Maurice can't prove that the part-time subcontract assemblers are all Outer Mongolian goat herders who come to work drunk on fermented yak[79] milk.
- John's ass will not be snatched to safety by his memos warning of suspect prototype test data because Bernie never got around to releasing the memos.
- Lawrence's engineering reports that cautioned that the Mark VIII was under-designed and over-promised were deemed erroneous then and are irrelevant now.

---

[79] Mo might be able to blow mare's milk past the CEO, but there's no chance he'll win with the yak milk.

What is relevant is that the buck gathers no moss on the CEO's desk. For the CEO it's all too simple. Our Guys are the softest target. Lawrence's head atop a ceremonial pole will be a very attractive sacrificial trophy and the cute little fringe of white hair will make it exceptional.

What do Our Guys need to do?

Make sure that they really have a problem

Lawrence has heard he has moved up to Position Uno on the CEO's Top 10 Fecal Compendium. Cy is said to be number 7, and both John and Mo made Honorable Mention. While rumors are rarely exactly true, if their names have ever been considered for the official HR Hatchet List, sure as hell they hold star billing on other lists, too. None of Our Guys will ever lead another task on a Rolls Royce project anywhere—and at DA, they'd need a work release from the corporate stockade to be a gofer on a Chevy Malibu retrofit project.

Decide about the rest of their lives

If they retire, Our Guys need to understand that it isn't what they are retiring from that matters, it's what they are retiring to. If they give up their work turf, they'll be on domestic turf where they hold minimal expertise, no seniority, and no more than minimal authority. Their job titles will plummet from guy in charge to incompetent assistant. The day may come when they are filled with green-eyed envy of The Village Old Fart.

If they decide to keep on working, they'll want to have something to do that they find to be rewarding, be it highly paying, highly satisfying, or highly fun. They may have to settle for keeping the wolf off the doorstep, though.

Ensure food on the table and roof over heads

Can money issues be ignored? No. Lawrence, Cyrus, and Maurice are eligible for meager retirements. Lawrence and Cy could scrimp along on their retirement checks, but their wives say no way. Maurice expects to live off his retirement and wife's salary until Social Security kicks in. John is in a tough spot—he'd get a thank you card and a gold-plated Timex if he bags it now. He needs to keep on earning. And inflation and health care can send anyone to the poor house.

Our Guys are on the bottom rung of the "Serves at the Pleasure of The Board of Directors" ladder with job security lasting through the current pay period. Their severance, retirement, unvested savings match, and stock options are at high risk. If the CEO has a bad rug morning on the day the shit happens, the peripheral bennies are toast and a lawyer's services will be needed to collect the last paycheck.

But how safe is the retirement money? DA has been a moderately successful company so it's unlikely to go bankrupt, but ironically this turns into a problem for Our Guys. The large bucks in the retirement vault make a tempting target in a hostile takeover, so retirees would be way better off to get a lump sum at departure instead of trusting the predatory company to continue to pay retirees their promised due.

Who will be in charge?

In the normal, sound, staff development case, the departing manager will have prepped at least one possible successor. But DA is not normal. It's common knowledge that nobody at DA messed up on the Mark VIII and many performed heroically.

There was no sandbagging either, but now, with E. Zelle the Weazelle guiding the hand of the CEO, Our Guys are going under the bus and most likely the best on-staff choices for their replacements will be blood sacrifices, too.

But wait! Before they take care of themselves, Our Guys need to take care of their staffs. E. Zelle and the CEO want lots of blood on the table. And even if the Weazelle gets moved up to a corner office, another of the CEO's apprentice toadies will be in charge. As a rule, in mass staff exfoliations, the strongest expelled personnel land on their feet. The middling type staff members who are not well networked in their field will need help. The erstwhile manager's connections will aid in finding work elsewhere for these middling guys, but there's no hope for the bottom enders. They are doomed to be triaged into the dustbin.

Lesson 16.2: If there ever is a time for bending the HR rule against giving the names of staff to headhunters, it's in the early days of a bloodbath.

Fast forward 1 year - how did it turn out?

Option 1: Sound the Charge!

When the fraud and failure news broke, the CEO went nuts and replaced Bernie by E. Zelle. Eager to wield his new power and never to be outdone in overreaction, E. Zelle exercised his bootlicker's prerogative and went nutser, screaming for a beheading.

Although Lawrence's staff had fixed every known Mark VIII bug as well as two more flaws they'd uncovered, the Mark VIII failed the reliability tests. In E. Zelle's eyes, Lawrence was accountable for working out the Mark VIII's bugs, so Lawrence was THE guy.

Sure that he'd get the axe if not sooner, then later, Lawrence grabbed the bugle and sounded the charge. He found another job before the axe could fall. He was only an okay engineer and at best an average manager, but he was well networked. A big push friend at Taytes (by then DA's chief competitor) arranged for Lawrence to be hired into Taytes. The Taytes job was nominally a no-better-than-lateral move, but for Lawrence it was way better than just okay. It utilized his major skills, the clean slate refreshed him, and Taytes' bright young staff stimulated his thinking. With the DA funk gone, he regained his energy and became a wise sounding board for the host of eager young innovators about him.

Lesson 16.3: It's good luck to have young friends who are smart, strong, and climbing their career ladders. It's even better good luck to have smart, strong friends in high places.

Lawrence knew that abandoning staff is the worst of all bridges to set aflame, so although he'd been screwed, he avoided the "screw you guys, every man for himself" thing. The staff of a manager who is leaving under a cloud is highly vulnerable to abuse by the new management and may get pushed out, too. Lawrence had to make time to write persuasive reference letters as he slipped out the door.

Lawrence was not being completely altruistic, though. He treated his reports fairly as he was pushed out the door, but he hoped that they'd remember if he needed their help somewhere down the road.

Lesson 16.4: When you are moving into a new job, who you know is more important than what you know. This is because what your new acquaintances think you know is way, way more important than what you know.

Meanwhile, back at DA, foiled by Lawrence's taking early retirement before a firing could take place, E. Zelle found need to lie a little to the CEO. E. Zelle claimed he'd "forced Lawrence into retirement". The CEO went to The Board and lied a lot, claiming that **he'd** fired Lawrence for cause and arranged for denial of all separation benefits. The Board was so enamored by the CEO's ruthless action that they declared the punishment complete and called off the Mark VIII-wide pogrom.

It wasn't the Board's intention at all, but calling off the purge saved a bunch of jobs by preventing E. Zelle from using the purge order as license to fire John, Mo, two Lawrence loyalists, and other players to be named. Thus, Lawrence's decision to get out before he was forced out turned into a benefit for Lawrence and everybody else in the department. Except E. Zelle.

Lesson 16.5: But in the end, it's always up to you to save your own ass. You can't count on someone else doing it for you. You have to snag good luck when it passes by.

There were downsides for Lawrence's job switch. He had to learn new systems, adjust to new staff, and lost his unvested 401k matches. He deemed it necessary to tweak DA noses by buying an upscale house to prove he was better off with Taytes, so he had a major mortgage expense. Further, he reverted to only two weeks of vacation. With greater *cojones*, imagination, and some brushing-up, Lawrence could have started a company selling his engineering knowhow. He would have needed some capital, too, but he already had the background and the connections for a niche market.

Lesson 16.6: Ironically, the average-to-mediocre, non-specialized guys like Lawrence do better at finding post-expulsion work in their fields than the smartest, highly specialized guys like Cyrus.

Remark: Cyrus was well known to be way stronger technically than Lawrence, but Cy was too specialized[80]. The top end science guys need sophisticated laboratories and costly equipment for their work while the middling types can make do with a laptop and a ball point.

Option 2: Hang on and hope for sunny weather

Reasoning that only Bernie and Lawrence were at risk in the Mark VIII debacle, Cy hunkered down to weather the storm. He averred to keep his nose clean and profile low.

Lawrence's early departure broke badly for Cy, though. Lawrence's replacement proved to be a suck-up and slacker. The new guy had no idea of how to do Lawrence's job so he botched everything. Then, as a manager will do when he doesn't know what he doesn't know, E. Zelle set out to fix all things via micromanagement across the entire staff, including Cy's section. Fearing CEO and E. Zelle reprisal, Cy held his tongue all the while. He was too busy saving his own ass to defend his staff.

Cy's top two guys had been getting calls from the headhunters, so they told Cy to shove it and left. The net reward for Cy's knuckling under was the loss of the strongest part of his staff.

Lesson 16.7: It's never a surprise when micromanaging sends the best guys out the door. Excellent experienced people get lots of good offers.

---

[80] "Too specialized" often means "Too damn smart for his own good."

Cy's section's productivity promptly fell off, so E. Zelle attacked Cy. Cy withdrew to a defensive perimeter. The big problem with don't-fight-back is that when you come under fire, the only way you can return any fire at all and yet appear to be cooperative is to somehow get your friends to stage a demonstration on your behalf. In theory, if enough supporting voices (other than yours) are raised, the Big Boys will hear and call off the dogs. This approach has two big flaws—you must have friends, and even more importantly, mounting a protest is tantamount to admitting that without lots of friends, you are utterly powerless.

Cy saw all this and set out to enlist staff support, but such a "Good luck, Cy—let us know how this turns out" moment it became! Because of his long history of being a cunning guy with an advantage-seeking management style, Cy had few dear friends among his fellow workers. Fervor in support of a benevolent manager who had been grossly victimized is rare. And fervor in support of a manager who had screwed over everyone he'd worked with at one time or another? By the end of the week, if Cy hadn't had Old Daisy the yellow Lab, he'd have had no friends at all.

Lesson 16.8: Protests on behalf of an egregiously wronged individual get good press, but protests go nowhere unless the protesters fear that they, too, will suffer the egregious wrong.

Option 3: Don't rock the boat and hope to be coaxed

John felt he had no choice but to continue doing what he was doing and hope he'd get a buyout. The only sure thing about letting the chips fall where they may is that the chips will fall. The CEO gets to choose the sacrificial lamb. Or maybe he'll choose a whole bunch of lambs and take no goats at all.

A year down the road, John has lost half of his best people and is still looking over his shoulder, hoping for a letter about a buyout, but fearing that instead of a lump sum, he'll be summoned to the gilded halls and dismissed with an ITR. (Individually Tailored Retirement, aka, Instantly Torn Rectum)

Option 4: Fight it

After Lawrence had saved everybody else's jobs, Maurice rededicated his life to research. Knowing that a little alcohol was good and a lot was bad, Mo spent his every leisure hour trying to find that elusive sweet spot where the bad didn't quite overcome the good. Sadly, though, again and again he overshot the mark and was forced to go work hung over.

Maurice decided that he was going to retire after all. He planned to spend a lot of nights at the bar, and since his wife still had to work, he could screw around on her from 9 to 5. But then he got to thinking about the thousands of dollars he'd lost because Bernie had banished him from management for seven years just because of the El Ranchito corner seat thing. The company owed him, big time. Mo had a score to even!

Mo conferred with a disbarred lawyer drinking buddy. The lawyer opined that Mo would never get a cent in settlement unless he could force DA management to choose between a modest settlement and a very deep pain event. The question then became: How could a current employee most effectively inflict pain on his management and yet avoid giving management a cause for firing?

Shaming management seemed the best idea to Mo. But how do you shame the shameless? In the midst of a fine drunk, martyrdom came as the answer. He'd kill himself.

Mo had this cool device in his garage—out on a community service trash pickup for a DUI conviction, he'd found an old-style instant tire deflator stop strip. The police had lost it during a cops vs robbers event on I-40 west of Albuquerque. Mo thought he'd drive his pickup over the stop strip at high speed, blowing both tires on the passenger side. The rusted-out pickup would roll and he'd be killed for sure.

Seeing that their long-lost stop strip had caused the problem, the cops would declare it an accident and the double indemnity in Mo's life insurance would pay off.

But even before he'd sobered up, the plan's flaws began to emerge: First, he was wronged by management, not the insurance company, so the "accident" would send no message to management. Second, he'd borrowed against his insurance and he was unsure that his insurance was even still in force because the payback process was murky and he was afraid to ask for fear of drawing attention to his scheme. Third, even if the insurance did pay off, his wife would just blow it at spas on wigs and hairdos.

And then it really happened. In the depths of rampant self-pity during his first first-rate drunk of the new year, Mo suffered a burst of insight. The CEO and E. Zelle and Bernie and Cy and Lawrence and even John and the whole fricking company had destroyed his career. He'd been reduced to a lesser man. Seppuku in public in front of his hated managers was the answer. Mo leaped from his bed and Googled Seppuku for Dummies.

Once billed as the only honorable way to face failure, seppuku fell victim to Japan's real estate credit bubble in the '90s. When the bubble collapsed, so much face was lost that the whole seppuku scene became banal and fell out of favor except in companies demanding total loyalty with respect to avoiding depleting the executive retirement trust fund. But that was in Japan, and Mo was in New Mexico.

Mo concluded that two rules in Seppuku for Dummies applied to him:

1. You must fearlessly fall on your sword in front of your critics.
2. You must tearlessly fall on your sword in front of your critics.

He'd show those bastards! At a general staff meeting, he'd boldly walk down to the dais, pull out his seppuku sword, plunge it into his chest, and cry out a single word, "Maria!".

Distraught, Maria would dash down and cradle his head against her beautiful bulging breasts. Amid her screams of anguish, she'd profess her love for him. With a trickle of blood oozing from the corner of his mouth, he'd gaze into her beautiful brown eyes and pass into eternity. Or were her eyes really black? Or maybe they were greenish? Shit, he didn't know. He'd never actually looked at her eyes because those other features had always caught his attention first.

He fell back asleep gloating about how he'd saddle those evil managers with pathos for the rest of their miserable lives — his blood, his agony, Maria's tears.

When he came to about noon, though, he realized a few details needed work. How could he get the sword past security? What if not all the evil, exploitative senior managerial villains were in attendance? Or suppose Maria does save his life, but he is brain damaged from loss of blood and nobody notices? And worst of all, what if the wrong Maria comes to his aid? He lusted for the young Maria with the big boobs, not the old one-night-stand typing pool Maria with the sour breath and crooked nose. She wasn't even an improvement over his wife.

The more Mo pondered, the surer it became that the melodrama card was a far better play. He'd fall on a virtual sword, and then courageously, yea, even theatrically, rise and silently vanish from their wretched lives forever. With the young and beauteous Maria at his side, he'd ride off into the sunset. His poignant departure would be burned into their memories forever. To hell with the severance. To hell with their retirement plan. To hell with finding another job! Faced with such a stirring image, Bernie and E. Zelle and the Big Boys would plead with him to accept restitution for the cheated thousands.

So, late on Friday afternoon, as Bernie was closing E. Zelle's general staff meeting, Mo leaped to his feet and snatched the mike from Bernie. Proclaiming that in protest for being unjustly demoted, he was resigning. Reading from the note card in his hand, Mo swore to reject any pitiable attempts by the company to buy forgiveness with a severance package. He was done. Right then and there!

Clapping loudly, Bernie turned to the audience, encouraging all to rise and applaud, too. Ripping the mike out of Mo's hand, Bernie shouted, "Congratulations, Mo! On your last day at work, you finally turned into a company man!" The "hurrahs" and "it's about times" were almost drowned out in the wild applause.

Dismayed, Mo faced the crowd. Dozens of hands waved bye-bye. In panic, he searched for his darling Maria. She wasn't there. Maybe she'd fled in anguish. She might have chosen to not answer her phone when he called to alert her about his planned drama. So, amid catcalls and complaints about getting the meeting over because it was way after quitting time, Mo stalked off the stage and out of the building, a disenchanted man.

Mo had been so sure of his performance that he had no plan B. Beyond drinking and screwing around, nothing appealed to him. He was a crappy golfer, he lost his ass every time he gambled, and his programming skills were obsolete so there'd be no call for temporary work. Retreating to the monastery at Abiquiu had seemed like a fine idea at one time, but the more he thought about celibacy, drinking homemade wine instead of booze, scratchy robes, and non-stop prayer, the less he liked that idea.

Lesson 16.9: Grandstanding loses its grandeur if the troops are glad to see you gone. And even if the majority are on your side, sympathetic voices tend to be soft and haters tend to be loud. Most managers will do better by fading away.

Mo took charge of his fate by becoming best drinking buddies with the disbarred lawyer. That lasted until his wife threw him out, so Mo showed her by dying from cirrhosis.

Bernie, ever coveting a bigger bonus, was thrilled that he'd ridded the company of Mo without the cost of a cent of severance or retirement money. But karma is a bitch. Handing out the bonus money was now E. Zelle's prerogative.

And then E. Zelle's karma became manifest; with the Mark VIII debacle taking DA into near insolvency, Taytes seized the moment with a deft unfriendly buyout. E. Zelle was rousted, and Jim, John's erstwhile supervisor at Taytes replaced E. Zelle.

With Jim in charge, John hung on until the kids were out of college and Social Security kicked in. He was a survivor.

Chapter 17
A Look Back

This short chapter revisits some important lessons drawn from the case studies in this book. Following the lessons, we'll cite some innovative management tools.

Highlights of Lessons

A number of lessons contained in this book seem worthy of repeating:

1.1: ...a widely utilized and very successful management tactic. If a guy stars at an ugly task, promptly reward him with a small bonus and assignment to several even uglier tasks.

1.4: Since senior managers believe they get paid to think of Good Big Ideas, they tend to think that everybody else thinks of Mediocre Little Ideas or Bad Big Ideas.

2.3: Any lie that keeps your boss' name off the police blotter is a good lie.

3.1: You can't depend on others playing fair just because you play fair.

4.2: The notion that a plan is a bit subversive lends great credibility to rumors.

5.4: Remember this when the shit hits the fan–your boss can always afford the better raincoat.

6.1: Once entrenched in a hierarchy, a dud manager can stink up the place almost forever if the higher-ups don't expect him to smell good.

6.3: If your goal is to rid your department of every high performing young lion except the fair-haired one, grooming an heir works even better than managerial selection via the eeny-meeny-miney-mo or rock-paper-scissors methods.

6.4: Being the last speaker is the best spot on the agenda, but only if you actually get to speak.

6.6: If you can transform a vague notion into a numerical score, you greatly improve your chances of convincing skeptics that the vague notion is factual.

7.3: To succeed in managing your manager, you must have a quid to provide, a pro to leverage your quid, and a clearly defined quo. To successfully leverage your quid, your pro must have a functional fulcrum.

7.4: However egregious they might be, weaknesses in performance are harder to exploit than weaknesses of the flesh. This is because failing performance requires extensive documentation, while assertions of lust have inherent credibility.

8.2: It took only two stinking errors to sink John. With a new system, you need zero errors to prevail in a conflict with an errant over-achiever.

11.1: All is lost if you don't hit the punchline.

11.2: Laughing on demand is a marketable skill.

12.2: Brevity is the greatest of all self-rewarding virtues.

13.3: What is the biggest barrier to women like Maureen? The establishment's belief that once a secretary, always a secretary.

14.1: Incompetent managers find it difficult to admit to their mistakes and even more difficult to take steps to correct their mistakes.

14.2: It's preferable to select promotion candidates based on their teachable skills rather than based on their overall job performance.

15.2: Let he who hires the loser, fire the loser.

15.3: When you listen to your gut, you gotta be careful about which sector of your gut is doing the talking.

15.4: Rank has its privileges. The boss can always be a bigger pissant than the subordinate.

15.5: If you have a guy who has had the desperate blues almost forever but suddenly perks up and says he's ready to take on the world, WORRY about him.

16.1: Senior managers like Bernie do not get fired for poor job performance. They get deposed when a higher power needs to demonstrate to a still higher power that "Steps are being taken to ensure …".

16.3: It's good luck to have young friends who are smart, strong, and climbing their career ladders. It's even better good luck to have smart, strong friends in high places.

16.4: When you are moving into a new job, who you know is more important than what you know. This is because what your new acquaintances think you know is way, way more important than what you know.

16.6: Ironically, the average-to-mediocre, non-specialized guys like Lawrence do better at finding post-expulsion work in their fields than the smartest, highly specialized guys like Cyrus.

16.7: It's never a surprise when micromanaging sends the best guys out the door. Excellent experienced people get lots of good offers.

16.8: Protests on behalf of an egregiously wronged individual get good press, but protests go nowhere unless the protesters fear that they, too, will suffer the egregious wrong.

Innovative Management Tools

A number of novel concepts are introduced in this book:

- A buzz phrase generator tailored for use in performance reviews (see Exhibit 2) and other documents requiring creative obfuscation
- An Economic model for managing your manager (see Chapter 4)
- The powerful Chemin de Fer Consensus Builder (see Chapter 6)
- In commemoration of the venerated Mohs Scale of Hardness of Minerals, we have developed two Mohs Scale extensions. These have proven to be indispensable management tools:
    1) The Moh's Hardness to Manage Scale (see Chapter 8)
    2) The Moh's Law of Personnel Performance Entropy (see Chapter 15)

We've come to the end of this book. We've had fun along the way and we hope you have, too.

We are pretty sure that having fun along the way is the important thing. Nobody gets out of life alive, so it must be the journey in life that matters and not the destination.

The End

About the Author

Noel Mohberg grew up in North Dakota, went to college at North Dakota State, grad school at Virginia Tech, and earned a PhD in biostatistics with a minor in epidemiology at the University of North Carolina. But hey, give the guy a break; nobody's perfect.

He worked at National Cancer Institute as a commissioned officer in the US Public Health Service, worked in rocket science at Sandia Laboratories, and eventually spent twenty-odd years as a manager in biostatistics and data management in pharmaceutical research and development. He then spent 16 years as a consultant in medical research.

He is a has been member of the American Amalgamation of Dull People, the Biometric Society, the American Statistical Association, and the Clinical Trials Society.

His previous publications include numerous papers in the medical and statistical literature, and two books, **Once You've Skinned the Cat, What Do You Do With the Pelt?** and **Letting the Cat out of the Bag is the Second Step**.

www.ingramcontent.com/pod-product-compliance
Lightning Source LLC
Chambersburg PA
CBHW060206070426
42447CB00034B/2701